THE Best Life EVER

ADITYA SHROFF

TreeShade Books

Published by TreeShade Books (VB Performance LLP) in 2019

THE Best Life EVER

ISBN : 9788193642481

Published by

TreeShade Books (VB Performance LLP)

Ansal Corporate Park, Sector142, Noida, Uttar Pradesh - 201305, India
Email - publish@TreeShadeBooks.com
www.TreeShadeBooks.com

Printed and Bound in India by
Thomson Press (India) Limited, 18/35 Delhi Mathura Road,
Faridabad – 121007 Haryana, India

Cover Design: Munisha Nanda
Typesetting: Ruchika Khanna

THE Best Life EVER

ADITYA SHROFF

TreeShade Books

www.treeshadebooks.com

To Fui,
who very early in life made me realise
that khakhra will always taste the best
when plastered generously with butter
and honey, and devoured with tales from
the Arabian Nights.

Foreword

Sometimes on warm summer afternoons, listening to the traffic-mingled sound of the sea in the distance, I find myself running my eyes over the rows of books in the shelf. It is a world full of thrillers and crime. Mystery and romance. Science fiction and fantasy. Action and drama. And looking out of the window, feeling the breeze on my face, I find one question pounding inside my heart.

Where are those Malgudi days?

And then one fine day, like a gust of fresh breath, these stories came along. All at once they put a smile on my face. Because it was a much-needed assurance from the universe that in a world that runs after materialistic happiness and trophies, there is still room enough to run merely for the fun of it. That if you wish for it to happen, the sun will still light up your eyes, the breeze will play with your hair and you will see how beautifully fulfilling a simple, healthy life can be.

And one foot-strike after the other, one step at a time, I someday aim to see a nation where health and wellness is as much of a priority as… breathing. And someday, with these fading footprints and memories, I hope to leave behind a fit world where people can afford to smile for the heck of it.

This book won't teach you how to run faster. However, it could perhaps subtly teach you… Life. If nothing else, these stories will show you that the spirit of humanity is still paramount and omnipresent. That emotions and memories still have a place in the heart.

And now I feel the ground under my feet and smell the wet soil in the air, and as I run with this village lad in spirit, I can assure you one thing. That like a fresh whiff of breeze, ladies and gentlemen, your Malgudi days have returned.

-Milind Soman

Inspired by real-life experiences.
By the magical landscapes of India.
By beautiful people with hearts of gold.
And by miles and miles of running.

Acknowledgements

'Ma, these are your ideas and your words. I am merely an instrument in the process. Make me write what you yourself would love to read...' Every morning when I would begin writing, this would be my prayer to Padma Ma, my spiritual Guru. She would smile back at me from behind the glass of the wooden-framed picture. And I will always believe that smile is where I found my inspiration. Thank you, Ma; this book is yours.

I thank Smita & Bhupat Shroff, my parents, for their unshakable, perennial support for whatever I have attempted in life so far—irrespective of whether or not I succeeded in it.

Growing up in a village where nobody speaks English, I thank Malti Shroff, Fui, for planting the seeds of the language in me.

Mansi Delannoy, my sister, for being a wonderful—and an indispensable—part of my childhood, glimpses of which make up this book.

If I were to name one person the book would have been absolutely impossible without, it would be Kasturi. My most important editor, the stories wouldn't have been half as gripping without her. The ultimate decision-maker, who helped me decide whether or not a particular sentence—or for the launch events, the blazer on my shirt—was necessary. But mostly, because she believed in the stories even when I didn't.

Heartfelt thanks to:

Dr. Arti Dastidar, for all the unconditional love, help, and ideas; for the thought-provoking vacations that have inspired parts of this book.

Frederic Delannoy, Mitali Dighe, Radhi Jangla De (and Ranadip De), Philip Earis, Pradip Khandwalla and Siddhartha Shah for their insightful editing and genuine feedback.

My agent, Dipti Patel, of Word Famous Literary Agents for kick-starting this beautiful journey and joining me alongside.

The entire publishing team at TreeShade Books: Vineet Bajpai for making the book come alive, Manisha Sobhrajani for the editing, Munisha Nanda for the cover design and Ruchika Khanna for the typesetting—and for putting up with all my last minute corrections.

Jagjit Arora for being a true elder brother; Jai Mani and Sonia Kulkarni for all their valuable support and mentorship.

Milind Soman for taking time out from his busy schedule for the Foreword.

Rukmini Thakur, Shalvi Saruparia, Aditya Pundir, Parthav Mistry, Vidit Panchal and Parth Bathia for being such great friends in times of need.

I deeply value every single compliment, comment and (constructive) criticism, be it on social media or otherwise; I can't put down all the names here, but it means a lot to me, for it encouraged me to keep trudging along this marathon journey.

And finally, I thank every single reader who picked up this book; nothing would ever work without your support. I hope you find as much magic in reading the stories as I found in writing them.

Contents

as far as you can see

'First left, then the second right, and you will be on the main street,' she tells me.

I stare blankly at the speaker. Her face—glowing much more than what is perhaps permitted at such an early hour—is smiling back at me, revealing a row of extremely white, perfectly polished teeth. Her jet black hair, tied back in a braid, again too perfect for this time of the day, is fragrant with coconut oil and glistens like a snake when she moves.

So thick is her south Indian accent that I understood nothing of what she said. 'Sorry, could you repeat that, please?' I ask her.

My host picks up a piece of paper lying on a small table—the only piece of furniture in the room—and draws what looks like a street map. I wait patiently as she adorns it with small arrows to mark out directions.

I look around the place, waiting for her to finish the sketch. It is a small room. A white curtain separates the kitchen from the living area, which doubles up as a bedroom at night. Smoky fragrance from a hand-rolled incense stick burning in one corner engulfs the dimly lit room. It stirs in my head some vague memories from childhood.

Happy memories. Like that small temple where Nana, my grandfather, used to take me each evening. They used the same incense sticks, didn't they?

I watch the fumes rise steadily from the burning stick, dance in the yellow light of the lantern hanging from the roof, only to coalesce peacefully into the surroundings, like they never existed. All that is left behind is the sweet perfume.

Perfume that brings Nana back to my side, hobbling with the support of his carved wooden stick towards the temple by the riverside.

In this small village, deep in the interiors of Kerala, for two hundred rupees a day, I have a mattress to sleep on, three full meals, and unlimited cups of black tea flavoured with home-grown cardamom. And to top it all, the lady of the house has promised to prepare my favourite sweet, *ela-ada*, once I am back from my run.

I first tasted ela-ada at a small tea shop in the marketplace. It is a rice pancake stuffed with freshly ground coconut and jaggery, and wrapped in banana leaf.

'Name?' I had asked, pointing at the sweets on display. In a place where nobody seems to speak more than a few words of English, I have taught myself to converse with vigorous hand gestures and a few accent-laced words. And it seems to work!

'Elaada,' the shopkeeper—a short, bald man, dressed only in a lungi—had replied.

'Ellayeda,' I repeated.

'No,' the shopkeeper shook his head. 'Elaada.'

'Elladaa?'

The shopkeeper shook his head again. 'Ela-ada. Elaada.'

I didn't understand what the deal was. Perhaps I couldn't mimic the accent. However hard I tried, I kept pronouncing it wrong. Finally, after eating to my heart's content, I had a helping of the sweet packed to take it along and show it to my host. When I told her how much I liked it, she promised to prepare it for breakfast the following morning.

She finishes the sketch quickly, and explains it to me in broken English that I can barely comprehend. I fold up the piece of paper and tuck it into my pocket, hoping I won't need it. However, I admit with a tinge of guilt that despite calling myself an adventure enthusiast, I do feel good (and secure) having a map handy!

I tell my host I will return after approximately three hours, in time for breakfast.

'Okay... elaada... ready,' she confirms with her trademark thumbs-up and a smile. That flash of white teeth against her dark skin lingers before my eyes as I make my way across the mud-plastered porch.

As I wave to her, her face does little to hide the fact that she hasn't quite understood why I need to go running. I have no explanation. In a way, she is right. I myself have never really understood why I go running. I wonder if I ever will.

I shut the woven bamboo gate behind me and step out into the darkness of the banana plantation. Treading gently, so as to keep the stillness of the early morning air intact, I duck between rows of banana trees, feeling my way past the slippery stems towards the open. The darkness is overwhelming and I wonder if I left a bit too early. It isn't the darkness, though; it is the uncertainty resulting from the darkness that unsettles me.

I decide to walk and not run until it is bright enough to see. With every step away from the house, fear begins to grip me. In this darkness, what if I step on a snake? A crouching scorpion? What about ghosts; do they really exist? There are stories of haunted trees in dark forests...

I hear a rustle behind me. My heart jumps to my throat. I stop dead in my tracks and turn around.

Nothing.

Only unfamiliar stillness in the fields surrounding me.

I can't help but notice the mystifying heaviness lingering in the air. As if I am being watched. Or followed. Like something is being forced upon me. Something opposing my stride. Like a set of hollow eyes looking at me with bated breath through the gigantic banana leaves. My imagination meticulously conjures up exactly those demons that I am most scared of.

I almost begin to retrace my steps, but there is only pitch darkness all around. The faint light from the house that had made its way through the gap in the leaves is long gone. A shiver runs down my spine. I keep walking with small hurried steps towards the end of the field, every muscle in my body tensed up and ready to explode.

After five harrowing minutes that seem like fifty, I am out in the open. The sky has begun to brighten up. The stars are fading. Faint outlines of the tall coconut trees begin to show. Another tiny house with a lantern hanging outside appears in the distance. I heave a sigh of relief. The fear evaporates. I laugh at myself for letting the darkness get the better of me. It is funny how the mind is scared of what cannot be seen. Simply because it cannot be seen. It is the uncertainty that is overwhelming. But sooner or later, the darkness recedes, and as always, the sun rises.

***

Once I get to the flat road, I break into a slow trot. The soil feels soft from the previous night's shower. There is a definite chill in the early morning breeze, and a light, grey mist hangs sleepily in the air.

The first left. Then the second right. And I am on the broad street leading up to the market. The directions are crystal clear. This is easy. I like the certainty. I jog through the sleeping marketplace. The empty street with its tarpaulin covered shops. The upturned stools and the extinguished bonfires. Not a soul in sight. It feels like the whole village suddenly decided to shut down. And I keep running through the ghost town.

Once out of the village, I take a quick look at the map. Then I turn left. I am now out of bounds; left to find my own way as the map goes no further. I should be scared. Instead, I experience an amazing sense of liberation: Running into the unknown at the break of dawn, in a land that doesn't speak my language, in a place that can hardly be called civilisation, amidst the Nilgiris! No expectations hold me back. No backpack weighs me down. Stripped down to just the bare necessities, I am a free spirit dancing in the hills, in the golden light of dawn. I breathe in the freshness of the cold morning air as I run past the nutmeg trees. A new place. An open road.

Very often, running brings about thoughts and emotions I never knew existed within me. And very often, I realise they simply cannot be put into words. Emotions like joy in the eyes of a lad who is done with the day's school, running down the street to the sweet shop. Or butterflies in the stomach that keep you up till dawn when your gaze meets hers for the very first time.

Thoughts that take me back to the fragrance of the incense stick in the temple as I glance over my shoulder at Nana's frail silhouette against the setting sun, to see if he is done praying and has opened his eyes, so I can run down to the river. The same peaceful eyes shut, as he lay motionless in his coffin. As if he is still in prayer. The wrinkles on his face lending it a beautiful character. The smell of burning wood replacing the sweet perfume of the incense sticks, as fire engulfs his worldly body. And his spirit flies free.

I run by silently as a wave of emotions washes over me. I am awed by the immaculate detailing in every single sentiment. The distinct flavour of life; at times, of death. Emotions so perfect and complete in themselves that I am almost scared I will ruin their tender, mellow fabric if I spend too much time dwelling on each. And so, I watch like a mere spectator as they pass me by.

I wonder how much courage one will need to even attempt capturing these feelings into words. It is meaningless, I decide. For emotions, like spirits, can't be caged. They soar free.

It seems like I have lost track of where I am going. But in this moment, it is too trivial an issue to let it override the exhilarating nostalgia.

Nana is talking to me. And so I keep running.

Daylight is fading as Nana and I walk back home. The incense stick has burned out. A few stars begin to appear in the sky. The genial evening has suddenly transformed into a surprisingly dark, moonless night.

'Don't go far,' I tell Nana, holding onto his walking stick. 'I can't see a thing ahead. I am scared!'

Nana merely laughs; a guffaw that turns into coughing, and takes some time to settle.

'Don't worry,' he tells me. 'You go only as far as you can see. When you get there, you will be able to see further. It is magic!'

It sounds alluring. I try it out. All I can see is the next few steps ahead. But when I am there, I can see the next few steps further ahead. I am delighted. It is magic, indeed!

'Promise me, dikra,' Nana's tone turns sombre, almost a bit alarmed. 'Promise me that you will never be afraid of the things you can't see. Just because you can't see them...'

I look into his deep eyes, intently looking into mine. He is tall and I have to crane my neck upwards to look at him. I can't make much of what he is asking me to promise, but I agree nevertheless. 'I promise, Nana.'

Nana smiles and pats me on the back.

As I run today, I am amazed at how much my brain remembers from the past. Or maybe it didn't really happen; my mind was simply making it up. Perhaps I had started believing it after playing it over and over a hundred times in my head.

I keep running between tea gardens on either side until the first rays of the sun illuminate the sky. Oh, the pristine beauty! The green carpet over the hills, and the forests in the backdrop. It is all so poetic and perfect, I almost feel guilty of intruding the space. I have no purpose being here, I think to myself. For being even a mere spectator here isn't an act. It is a privilege; an honour. The sheer glimpse of the grandeur stretching out before me makes me want to jump in joy. To laugh out aloud. To run faster than ever. Purely from the feeling of breathing and being alive in this panorama.

The world seems to be gently stirring awake. The tea-pluckers mark colourful dots on the sea of green, making their way around the tea gardens, like tiny, coloured caterpillars gnawing away at a giant leaf.

A group of young school boys point at me and laugh. My running shorts are probably too short. Or my bright red jersey a bit too bright. I would never be able to blend in. No.

A tea vendor pours a glass from his steel kettle for an early customer, letting out a puff of steam infused with the aroma of cardamom so pure that it makes me want to stop and have a cup. I breathe in deeply, stealing all that I can from the rejuvenating fragrance as I pass by.

Soon I should be reaching back 'home'. I am hungry. I can almost taste the elaada in my mouth. The delicate texture of tender coconut, the dark golden, molten mass of jaggery, enhanced by the flavour of the banana leaf; it has me drooling.

But then something strange happens. As I take the final right that should have led me to the marketplace, I realise to my horror that I am nowhere near the market. Instead, the right leads me yet again along a narrow trail, one that disappears into the forest. Startled and disoriented, I pause for a moment to examine my surroundings. Did I pass through this place on my way out? I can't tell. I retrieve the map from my pocket. It is damp with sweat. Carefully, I unfold it and look through the arrows marked. It doesn't help. The roads are nothing like the ones marked on it. Where could I have gone wrong? Maybe it is the next right turn, I think to myself.

But the farther I run, the more I am convinced that I am on the wrong path.

I see a passer-by and stop.

'Market?' I ask him.

He shakes his head. He doesn't understand English. After a couple of tries, I finally meet someone who does.

'Market?' he asks me right back, desperately searching his seemingly limited English vocabulary for words. 'Big distance... ten kilometres...' he points in the opposite direction.

What!

I stand there for a moment, as the world spins around me. I have lost all sense of direction and orientation now. Where on earth am I? Just to be sure, I stop again next to a group of tea-pluckers and ask them the way to the market. It causes some commotion within the group. They seem to discuss something. 'Which market...?' one of the women finally asks me.

Which market? WHICH MARKET?

What do they mean? How would I know the name of the market!

A young woman in her early twenties proceeds to explain. Her English is incoherent and doused with a strong accent. Moreover, she starts off in English and soon slips into a steady stream of Malayalam, until I stop her and ask her to start all over again. Finally, after a few retakes, what I gather is that there are two markets in two different directions from where I am standing. Lost as I am, I want to spare myself the embarrassment of looking like a fool before a group of women, and run out of their sight preferably before they start giggling at my shorts. Trying my best to hide the pangs of panic beginning to appear on my face, I thank the tea-pluckers and proceed in an arbitrarily picked direction, as if I know exactly which market I want to get to.

In reality, I am anything but confident. There is a new dimension to my uncertainty as I stand between—and far away from—two unfamiliar markets, not even knowing the name of either. I neither know which direction to take to either of the markets nor do I speak the local language. What makes my predicament worse is that there is not a single penny in the little damp pocket of my running shorts!

I begin to palpitate with fear, partly from the twenty-five kilometres I have just run and mostly from sheer nervousness. I can feel my legs trembling under me.

There's more: I can't even seem to recollect the name of the village I am putting up in. Chithipuram? No. Idukki? No, that is the name of the district! Anaviratty? Pothamedu? Why couldn't they have simpler names? A dozen signboards I had read earlier, each with half a dozen names, pop up in my head. These could be places miles away from here. Places I had passed on my way the previous day using some of the most bizarre modes of transport. From a jam-packed, rattling, state-run bus that was almost falling apart, to sharing a ride with two goats and a farmer on a bullock cart, to crossing a lake on a boat that doubled up as home for a family of eight. All this and I wasn't even a wee bit scared. Because I had my backpack. I had money. A phone. The Internet. Certainty; I had certainty.

And here I am, all alone, accompanied only by a grumbling tummy and a pair of tired legs. Helpless, I am on the verge of breaking down. Somehow I collect myself and decide to run down to either of the markets and find help. I have been lost before, I tell myself. I can handle this.

I make my way through the snaking trail of the lush green rainforest. The dewdrops have dried, but the freshness is intact. In different circumstances, I would have longed to run my fingers over those shimmering diamonds. However, today I don't care. I want to get home. I want definite directions. I want certainty.

The tall eucalyptus trees are beckoning. It is a beautiful sight. The feeling of being in the woods is amazing. But not today. Today it is lonely and uncertain.

Despite half-an-hour of tense running, I am nowhere close to the end of the woods. The dense vegetation shows no hint of thinning down, just like the narrow trail that betrays no sign of giving way to civilisation. It only seems to get thicker, to a point where the canopies completely block out sunlight. More than anything, I am now scared of wild animals. Of all the ways there are to die, I don't want to be hunted down!

I am running faster than ever, casting a cautionary look behind me every now and then, watching out for springing panthers. In a way it feels like running a race, looking over the shoulder for signs of fellow competitors, and yet it is a different feeling altogether. Running for a trophy could never match the intensity of running for your life, could it?

Right now, more than anything else, I want to get out of here. Alive. The sight of the trail is the only motive pushing me forward. I hang on to it like it is my lifeline.

The darkness in the woods seems to be getting darker, and I realise it is going to rain soon. From the gaps in between the trees, I see clouds overhead. Dense, dark clouds. Dark as the brow of my host who is probably waiting for me back home. I remember her flashing white smile. She had simply shrugged when I had asked if she thought it would rain today. I had assumed she hadn't understood my question. In reality, this is the funny part about the weather in these equatorial hills. You can never tell how the day will turn out to be. It could be sunny with blue skies and small white clouds when you step out, and you could get caught in a thunderstorm the next hour and come back home drenched.

As I run along, every single step seems uphill. My legs are a pulp. Even at an easy pace, my heart rate is soaring and I am breathing hard.

And then the rain comes pouring down. There is no gentleness to it, no drizzle as a warning sign, and there is no time to look for a shelter. It is torrential; it comes down like a waterfall from the heavens. As if someone had punched a gaping hole in the clouds. A gasp escapes my lips as the surprisingly cold rainwater runs down my back. In no time, I am drenched to the very bones. My jersey sticks to my skin, begging for the comfort that I, in turn, ought to be seeking from it.

I pause to catch my breath. I am shivering. I bend over to stretch my hamstrings. They are stiff as ever. And what I see forms a lump in my throat. There are half-a-dozen black gooey insects sticking all over my bare legs.

Leeches!

Hurriedly, I pluck them all off. Blood starts trickling down my legs. It doesn't hurt; leech bites never hurt. But it is the sight of the freely flowing blood that breaks me down.

My stomach heaves. The leeches manage to shatter the last bit of courage holding me together. I want to scream.

The rain ceases sooner than I had anticipated, looking at its intensity. But that isn't the end. Slowly, but surely, the range of my vision diminishes as fog creeps into the forest. It is so typical: thunder, then rain, and then fog. It comes like a wave and I am forced to stop running. It becomes so dense, engulfing me completely, so much so that I can barely see the tree in front of me.

'I am scared,' I say to Nana. 'I can't see a thing ahead!'

That same old, familiar, ringing laughter.

'Don't worry,' he tells me. 'You need to go just as far as you can see...'

I look into his old, smiling eyes, brimming with the courage of a lion. Eight decades worth of courage!

'...and when you get there, you will see the way ahead. It is magic!'

It is magic, I repeat to myself over and over again. Like a chant. An incantation. It is magic, indeed. Nana smiles.

I begin to take one step after the other. I will keep going as long as I can see the trail under my feet, I decide.

Twenty minutes later, I am out in the open. It feels much better than the woods, but it doesn't solve my problem. The place is still unfamiliar. I consider going to a local police station for help. But I give up the idea, thinking I will only make a fool of myself because I don't know where I came from in the first place. On the other hand, what if they made a big deal out of it, and my host—the kind, smiling lady—throws me out of the house fearing trouble? I rule out approaching the police and keep walking, hoping to find some locals. My hungry tummy grumbles in protest. I think about the elaada waiting for me. The thought of it, followed by cardamom tea, makes my mouth water.

And then a wild idea strikes me. The shop where I had eaten elaada was the only shop in the neighbourhood that prepared it. 'You don't get this anywhere else,' the bald shopkeeper had told me, his chest swelling with pride. 'Only here. Elaada... only here!'

If that were true, I have a chance. I begin running again with renewed energy. I see an old man in a lungi cycling up the road and rush to him, almost scaring him off the bicycle.

'Elaada?' I ask him. And then, using aggressive hand gestures, I try my best to simplify the English: 'I… want… to… buy…elaada!'

The man doesn't understand. He shakes his head and begins to mount his bicycle.

'No... Please... One moment, sir...' I stop him desperately. 'I. Want. To. Purchase. Elaada.' I speak slowly and clearly.

Still no reaction.

'Ellayeda...? Yellaada? Ellaa-yeda?' I try all different pronunciations and accents, holding back desperate tears of helplessness, my voice trembling.

'Ella...?' he looks puzzled.

'Ellada... banana leaf... shop selling Ellayeda. Yellaada!' I act out the banana-leaf wrapping with my palms.

To my delight, his eyes light up. 'Ah, elaada!'

'Yes! Yes! Ellayeda!' I stop myself just short of hugging him.

He lets out a short toothless chuckle, followed by a stream of words in Malayalam, repeating the word 'elaada' a couple of times, obviously telling me how I had pronounced it incorrectly. Waving my hands, I ask him which way I should go, hoping he will understand. He shakes his head, motioning forward along the road, probably trying to say it was far away. That didn't matter. The distance was no longer an issue, as long as I had the right direction.

'Elaada shop... This way...?' I ask to confirm.

He nods, but with a degree of apprehension.

I am about to begin walking when he points at the back carrier of his bicycle and says something I don't understand. It takes me a while, and then I get it.

Soon I am seated behind this unknown bicycle guy, clutching his lungi to avoid falling off, headed (hopefully) in the direction of (hopefully) the sole elaada shop in the area. A dozen thoughts and uncertainties dance around in my head, wreaking havoc. A dozen unanswered questions. Had the guy understood me right? What if there *was* another elaada shop, after all? What if I was actually going further *away* from 'home' on this bicycle?

The steel bars of the carrier dig into the flesh of my behind. Every bump in the stony road makes me clench my teeth. And all the while I head into the boundless uncertainty with my old lungi-wearing Malayali friend.

I can't help but notice how similar to Nana he looks from the back. The same frail structure, the half bald head, the trimmed white hair at the back.

It is magic. It is magic, indeed.

I crane my neck to peep ahead along the road. Partly to prepare myself for the next pothole on the way, partly to see if the surroundings begin to look familiar, and partly to see if it really is Nana riding the bicycle! After an excruciatingly long ride, to my utter disbelief, relief, and joy all put together, I see the shop in the distance. That very shop! Spent as I am, it makes me want to dance in sheer delight, and cry for joy.

Thanking the old man profusely, I try to explain how guilty I feel for not having anything to offer him in return for his generosity. I can feel the sting of tears in my eyes. The tears of relief. Of happiness. Of exhaustion. Of self-pity. But mostly of gratitude.

He wipes his dark, wrinkled brow now beaded with sweat. It must have been hard pedalling up the unpaved road with a heavy guy on the back carrier weighing the bicycle down. A soft smile appears in his eyes. I don't know if he understands how much I want to return his favour. But looking into those eyes, I can be sure that he expects nothing from me in return.

I want to embrace this old bicycle man. I want to tell him how much his help means to me. I want to explain what I have been through. How he has saved me in this strange place far away from home. But language fails me. Even if it hadn't, I realise, words would have been too shallow to convey the indebtedness. So I am content—content in simply standing there with moist eyes, watching him slowly cycle out of sight.

'Thank you, Nana,' I whisper.

The frail, half bald figure, with trimmed white hair at the back, disappears into the distance.

***

Sunlight streams into the little room, illuminating the place with a warm glow. I sit by the window overlooking the banana plantation, dreamily sipping on hot cardamom tea. A rice pancake stuffed with jaggery and coconut sits on a banana leaf before me. Elaada, I smile to myself, knowing for certain I have pronounced it wrong.

I go through the morning's events in my head all over again, wondering if they had really happened. It seems like a dream. But the enduring ache in my legs and my wet clothes hanging on the clothesline by the window remind me it was all for real. I look outside, as miles and miles of rows of banana trees stretch out before me. I think of how far I have come, from the time I was still a little boy walking alongside Nana.

I think of how far I want to go in life.

But I can see nothing ahead.

'Don't worry,' Nana touches me on the shoulder, 'you need to go just as far as you can see...!'

And then I join him.

'...and when you get there, you will be able to see ahead. It is magic!' We finish together in perfect synchronisation.

The incense stick burning in the corner makes me want to reach out and hold Nana's hand. It is magic.

I bite into the goodness of the jaggery-coconut filling. It is magic.

I will never go out so far on unknown roads, I tell myself. And then I suddenly remember the promise I had made to Nana as a small child walking next to him through the darkness. *Promise me that you will never be afraid of the things you can't see. Just because you can't see them...*

I shut my eyes and think of him. 'I promise, Nana.'

Nana is smiling. With ostensibly effortless motion, he reaches out with his beautifully wrinkled hand, and pats me on the back.

The hand-rolled incense stick in the corner burns sweeter than ever.

***

the price of a coconut

My parents moved to the countryside when I was just a few months old. It is a quaint little coastal town called Umarsadi. A town so tiny, it doesn't even exist on the map of India. A town so inconsequential, it doesn't even need to. But like a dot on the western coastline bordering the Arabian Sea, it sits amongst the tall, silent coconut groves by the shore. I have grown up on a farm. A farm for a playground, and a few hundred coconut trees as my sole playmates. I have been raised on coconut water, sunshine and the summer breeze. My relatives from the city are of the opinion that had I grown up in the city, I would have been a different person altogether. I agree. I wouldn't have been quite as alive!

I have faint memories of swinging on a white netted hammock tied between two coconut trees. I remember trying to escape a stray sunbeam that would make it past the coconut canopy and onto my face, as the occasional breeze from the sparkling sea gently rocked the hammock.

In retrospect, I laugh at how I imagined the sun as an enemy trying to shoot at me through the trees with its blinding beams, until one day when my mother told me that my name meant the sun, in Sanskrit. It felt strange to think that up in the sky, I was my own enemy.

I didn't understand it then. But I do now. I do, when I am pushing hard on a run. When all I want to do is just give up. That is when I realise that nothing in the world wants me to stop, more than my own self. That I am indeed my own enemy.

Over the last twenty years, nothing about my playground has changed: the same tall trees, the same muddy trails beaten down between them, and the same canopy roof above. The place still means the world to me for I mostly run here; and so, the most sacred part of my day is spent in these coconut groves.

Nothing seems to have changed except the price of coconuts. A few years ago, each coconut fetched us four rupees; now they fetch us nine. People from the city say they buy coconuts at thirty-five rupees a piece. I wonder where the rest of the money goes!

In any case, nine rupees is a good price. Nine is a perfect number. For when a thirsty patron comes to buy a coconut for nine rupees, you sometimes get to keep ten when he doesn't have loose change. Ten rupees and a friendly chat in the shade of the trees, until he is done drinking: an amazing deal, I would say.

***

The sun is still lingering over the horizon at the edge of the farm as I finish my run. I pick out a large green coconut from the heap of harvested coconuts patiently waiting for the pick-up to arrive and carry them to the market. Sometimes I, too, wait for that farm truck just as intently—listening to its engine, and the sound of its wheels skidding in the mud before finding dry ground to roll on. The smell of half-burnt diesel fumes brings back pleasant memories.

When I was a young boy, I fancied luxury cars and fast sports cars. But as I grew up, I realised I liked them only because the world liked them. I am glad I came to the realisation that nothing gladdens my heart as much as the roar of that country pick-up. Let the world say what it must, my father would always tell me. Stay true to your ways of happiness. Be proud of them. And for once, never ever forget where you came from.

Oh, how could I ever forget this coconut farm! The afternoons spent lying in the hammock; the evenings spent running between rows of coconut trees. And there isn't a better feeling in the world than to have this sweet, naturally cooled tropical elixir run down my parched, thirsty throat after a summer run! I sit on the heap of coconuts, sipping from the biggest of the lot, looking at the setting sun hanging like a giant, shining coconut from one of the trees.

And then I see them. Towards the edge of the farm, I spot two young men. One of them has climbed halfway up a tree. The other one is waiting below. I strain my eyes against the sun's rays to look. Who could it be? I look at the watch. It is past five and the workers have finished work for the day. And then it hits me: coconut thieves!

My heart starts to race. My natural instinct asks me to raise an alarm. But I realise that they will escape before somebody responds. I know what I should do. Slowly, I start creeping towards them, sprinting from tree to tree and then hiding behind a trunk to catch my breath before the next sprint. I peep from behind the trunk. One of the guys is keeping a watch, while the other is busy plucking coconuts and dropping them down to his accomplice. I feel my blood boil. *My* coconuts. *My* farm. The fruit of years' worth of sweat and toil. How dare they steal!

I am still about a hundred metres from them. If I make even a small mistake now, I will give them more than enough room to escape. I can feel my heart thud in my ears as I creep closer. One more sprint to the next tree. Eighty metres. Still unnoticed. Phew! I feel like a crouching lion getting closer to his prey.

Sixty metres. My heart is banging against my head now. For a split second, I wonder if the lion might be equally nervous just before pouncing on the prey. I guess not. I guess he would go all out, wouldn't he? Fearless. All guns blazing. Get the prey or starve to death. And that is why most often he makes it; he gets the prey. That is what makes him the king of the jungle.

But me? No, I am a coward jackal. Fifty metres. I swear I could have wet my pants. My breathing is so loud I am scared I will be heard.

And then I am heard. And seen.

The accomplice raises an alarm and starts sprinting at lightning speed as his partner on the tree slides smoothly down, like a perfectly trained peasant who had climbed a thousand coconut trees. Or perhaps lived on one his entire life.

And I am left standing there. Too dumbstruck to react. Too nervous to even take a step. Like at the start of a difficult race, trepidation and imaginary pain paralysing the senses; locked, jammed, legs shivering, heart exploding, the stomach so uptight I could collapse in a heap right there.

Somehow I manage to recover and find the courage to chase. Letting out a threatening cry, I erupt into a sprint. It seems like I might lose them. They have already run past the last row of coconut trees and into the adjacent farmland, their slender frames gliding away over the undulating ground, their quick unshod feet prancing effortlessly over the loose rocks.

But I am the hungry lion. Hungry and angry. Putting in the last bit of strength, I follow. Opening up my stride and sprinting, I only have one point of focus in the distance. I've got my eyes set on the prey but they are swift and agile; tough, hard-core peasant blood. Moreover, if I were running for my prey, they were running for their lives. If I fail, I would simply go back angry. But they? They didn't have the luxury of such a choice. If they failed, the consequences would be severe.

I try raising an alarm. No response. My frantic calls fade away into the open fields like the faint grassland breeze, barely making even the blades of grass rustle. The question is whether or not I will be able to hold my sprint longer than they can hold theirs. The answer seems more and more certain with every step I take. I am beginning to sink. My body is giving away. It has been almost three whole minutes of chasing them. And this, after a hot summer evening run!

But then something happens. As the second thief follows the first, jumping over the barbed wire fence in a hurry, he trips and goes flying face down to the ground. This is my moment! He manages to get back up but before he can flee, I pounce on him, grabbing him by the collar and pulling him down. In the spur of the moment, and in a fit of rage, I raise my fist and smash it over his face. A cry escapes his mouth. He looks at me, stunned. I am still breathing hard, ready to collapse from the intense chase. I manage to sputter some angry words, futilely incoherent. Words that sound more like gasps of air.

And then a cold shiver passes down my spine. The accomplice is gone, but the guy in front of me looks like he will put up a fight! The prey I had just pounced on could well turn out to be my predator!

How did I never expect this to happen? I am alone, and so is he. But he certainly is the stronger one. I am in no condition to put up a fight. I am exhausted to my very core. And he looks lean and ripped. Before I have time to think, he flings his fist towards me. I am caught unaware. It lands hard on my nose. The blood in my head spirals. Tears form in my eyes from the blow. I feel warm blood trickle down my lips.

'Chor! CHOR! Thief! THIEF! Is anybody there...?' I call out desperately.

Only the leaves rustle in excitement.

'Kalpesh...? Thakor...? Kalpesh...?' I call out to the farm workers.

No response. They are all done for the day, I recall. They have all probably gone back home by now. I wish I had carried my phone with me for the run. Or a stick at least. Out of sheer trepidation, I pounce on him. We grapple on the hard ground for a while. My shoes have come undone. He tugs at my collar, and I hear a few stitches of my jersey give way. Then with a stroke of luck, I manage to land a hard blow on his tummy. Knocked out of breath, he doubles over. Before he can recover, I strike again. And again. My knuckles hurt. But that is all I can do. I am suddenly driven by fear, not anger. And fear, they say, bites more vehemently than fury.

Finally, the young man gives in. He can barely breathe. Sitting crumpled on the ground, he starts pleading and whimpering. '*Maaf kari do, Bhai, bhool thai gai*!' Forgive me, Bhai, I made a mistake. 'Please let me go... I swear on my mother I will never come back here, Bhai...'

'Why do you steal in the first place?' I bellow. The fear gets instantly replaced by anger. By authority. The authority of a farm owner.

'We were hungry, Bhai...' he wails.

'Shut up! I don't want your lies. And IF YOU EVER COME BACK....' I point a finger into his face, sounding more threatening than I intend to.

'No, Bhai... Never...'

I give him one more shove as he scurries away. I watch him disappear out of sight like a tiny farm rat, and then begin walking back home. Proud. Excited. Equipped with a story to tell the world. But first I must escape from here. What if they return with a gang merely out of vengeance?

My pace increases. A slow trot first. Then a jog. Then finally I break into a run. And as I run, I can't help but think. I can never quite seem to understand why my thoughts always feel much more lucid when I run. For some reason, at the intersection, I don't take the right leading back home. Instead, I keep running straight through the teakwood forest.

We were hungry, Bhai... I keep thinking of the thief's words as I run.

You denied a hungry man food. A small voice in my head starts talking.

But he was a thief...! I try to reason.

And as if that wasn't enough, you beat him up. The tiny voice is unrelenting.

He needed to be shown what's right and what's not. And he tried to attack me... I argue.

Who started it, asks the voice. *Oh, and you think you get to decide who's wrong and who's right? All this after denying him food? Isn't THAT a bigger sin than theft? All this for nine rupees? Is that what a few coconuts are worth? Is that the price of a coconut for you?*

I start running faster to cut out the voice. But it follows.

We were hungry, Bhai... The voice keeps playing in my head. I speed up in an attempt to run away from the voice. I am trying to break free from the scruples of conscience.

We were hungry, Bhai...

I am almost sprinting. My hand feels swollen from the punches. The fingers are red and puffy. Even a gentle shake makes my right palm hurt. It hurts even more when I swing my arms to and fro as I run. I clench my fist. The swelling makes me wince in pain. Good. I clench it harder. It makes me run harder.

We were hungry...

I suddenly reach a tipping point. No matter how hard I run, the voice follows. For the voice is inside me. I am that voice, I realise. And I possibly can't run away from myself. I am still carrying that dirty heart with me. Bleeding black with savagery. The brutal heart that denied a hungry man food, and beat him up. I am devastated. I stop running at once.

I keep looking at the fading sun for a long time, weeping. That same bright ball that used to shoot at me through the trees. Today, again, I am reminded the hard way that I am my own enemy. Humanity is dead. And I am left standing alone with the heap of harvested coconuts at my feet, just after having desperately scrimmaged for a few. Oh, the irony! I have never felt so lonely. I am ashamed. With the sleeve of my jersey, I wipe away a tear threatening to slide down the corner of my eye.

The sun has set. Here I am, facing my thoughts, and my heart, weighed down by guilt. Was this the price two hungry men should pay for a few coconuts? Were nine rupees worth all this for me? I will never be able to explain how, but somewhere this is what running has made me: a bit too soft; a bit too fragile; a bit too human. I wish I could go back and offer those hungry men a coconut or two. I wish I could tell them they didn't need to steal anymore.

But they are gone.

***

Two years have passed since.

But even to this day, when I finish my run, I stand facing the setting sun, coconut in hand, scanning the horizon to see if the hungry thieves are back. Hoping against hope that today I will correct the wrong. Hoping that I can promise them that in this world, humanity and compassion rank higher than this heap I am sitting on. That they are worth much more than the price of a coconut.

I am still waiting. The thieves have never returned.

For some reason, coconut water never tastes the same after a run anymore.

And nine rupees never felt so heavy in my pocket before.

***

# of Himalayan wildflowers

I wonder if I will die.

Huddled next to my sleeping bag, Kavyaa wonders the same. The more she tries to banish the thought, the more it seems to come back. Deep in her heart, like a ray of light pouring into a cold, dark room through a tiny crack, she believes I will pull through. But with every passing hour in the tiny tent, and the sound of the rain pouring with increased vehemence, the delicate flame of hope in her heart begins to flicker. That crack letting in the warmth of hopefulness seems to recede. Until the cobwebs of doubt shut out the light completely.

Suhas Bhaiya, our unfailing guide-cum-cook, who, the previous day, had merely laughed off my doubts about whether or not I would make it back alive to the base camp, now seems exceptionally silent.

'Will he be fine?' Kavyaa whispers to him in a hushed tone for the tenth time in two hours.

He does not laugh this time. Like our tiny tent in the gusty winds, his confidence, too, seems to be wavering. I can sense it even with my eyes shut. He takes twice the amount of time to answer, his tone a lot softer. And even though I am not looking at him, I know he is speaking without making eye contact with Kavyaa. Does he think I might not pull through?

'He will be fine...' Suhas Bhaiya stammers. Then, in an almost inaudible tone, as if muttering to himself, he adds: '...if the rain stops.'

'When will the rain stop?' Kavyaa asks immediately, her voice heavy with despairing hopelessness. Yet hoping, desperately hoping, that this mountain man could look at the darkness of the clouds in the sky and magically work up a formula to tell her exactly when the rain would stop. Or maybe even work up his magic and stop the rain.

But Suhas Bhaiya remains silent. He had not expected the rain to last for more than four or five hours. 'Six at the most,' had been his words. But it has now been thirty-five hours. Thirty-five hours! And the rain betrays no sign of slowing down.

Stranded amidst the enormity of the Himalayas, with a tiny tent to protect us from nature's fury, I lie in my sleeping bag, severely dehydrated from an extreme bout of diarrhoea that I contracted about twenty-four hours ago. We can't reach even the closest town because the rain has made the trail extremely dangerous, even for someone completely fit and healthy. Suhas Bhaiya says the stream that we crossed on our way up from the base camp would now have swelled up and become so forceful it would sweep us miles down into the valley if we even set foot into it. He says it will be impossible to cross it until the rain stops and the water from the hills has finished flowing down the slopes.

Half awake and half asleep, my body partly conscious, and partly in a painful trance, I listen to the relentless pattering of the rain against the plastic sheet that Suhas Bhaiya covered the roof of the tent with when the rain became too fierce for the tent's fabric. That drumming of the rain on the plastic takes over everything. The overwhelming sound fills the tent, fills our ears, beats with our heart, even runs in our blood. And in all honesty, it acts as a reminder that I am still alive. And yet like a corpse staring at the yellow roof, I lie—half alive and half dead.

Nothing has stayed inside my stomach for more than thirty minutes. It has sunk to form what I see as a depression, as I lie on the cold, damp floor. Every few minutes debilitating cramps hit me, and the pit in my stomach seems to get deeper. That intense vacuum in the guts gives me the feeling that it is only a matter of time until I will be completely sucked inside. The spasms come and go, in some mysterious synchronisation with the howling winds outside, increasing and decreasing in intensity every few minutes. They come by with ferocious gusto, finally having decided to sweep the poor tent away. And just like that, if I did survive the stomach cramps this time around, it just feels like a matter of minutes until the next set of spasms come along. And take me away. For good. Like the frail little tent.

I listen to Kavyaa fumble around in her bag, checking and rechecking a dozen times to see if any of the medicines remain. Rinifall. O2. Even a crocin. Or one of those rehydrating electrolyte sachets we packed. But they have all been used up. Only the crumpled wrappers remain. Only the deceitful crunchy sound of the empty plastic bags.

'I need to go,' I whisper to Kavyaa, my voice barely able to rise above the sound of the wind outside.

'Again?' she sighs.

Again. Yes, again. Seventh time in three hours, I make a mental calculation. Or is it the eighth or ninth? Who knows! A dying man is hardly good with numbers.

Yesterday, I had the energy to go behind a bush a bit away from the tent. But since this morning, I have barely been able to get onto my feet. Kavyaa hands me the umbrella as I put on my rain jacket. I open the tent flap and stumble out of the tent, my windcheater scarcely holding up against the strong winds. It is freezing outside. Probably five degrees Celsius.

The sky is still overcast. Two steps to the side. That is all I can muster. Gripping the umbrella firmly between the shoulder and my cheek, I unbutton my trousers and pull them down. Cold droplets of rainwater whip against my bare skin, sending a chill up my spine. Directing the umbrella against the wind current, I squat, and everything that is supposed to come out—and everything that isn't—comes gushing out of my rear. I realise that all I am dumping out is water. I feel so empty as if there is nothing left inside, except the intestines. Who knows, the next time I might lose them as well. I don't need a toilet paper roll. The torrential rain lashing my behind does the job for me.

With nothing left in me, I swing open the flap of the tent, get back inside and collapse onto my sleeping bag. The ground feels colder than before. The water seems to be seeping in from below. We are all freezing inside the tent. The diarrhoea will kill just me, but the cold will kill us all, I think to myself. Sitting beside me with her chin tucked between her knees, I can feel Kavyaa's body shivering silently. I feel sorry for her, as much as I do for myself. Until yesterday, we had been using the flame from the portable cooking stove to heat up the tent. But when the rain refused to cease, Suhas Bhaiya declared we were running out of kerosene. We needed to make a choice: between using the last reserve of kerosene from the carboy to either heat us or to feed us. We mutually decided to hang on to the last bit of hope: hope that the rain would stop and the sun would shine. We decided to freeze instead of starve.

In the middle of nowhere, there are a dozen ways in which things can go wrong. Or call them ways to die—the diarrhoea, the cold, the rain, running out of food, and a whole lot of other unexpected troubles that the angry Himalayas might throw our way. For example, Suhas Bhaiya's mule, Raja, who had carried our luggage, tent and food up the mountain, trekking for two whole days, has not been sighted since the past few hours. Suhas Bhaiya says he can't be far, and that he is probably only taking shelter from the heavy rains. But then Suhas Bhaiya had said a lot of other things that turned out to be outright wrong. The Suhas Bhaiya that we had trusted as we set out for the trek doesn't seem to be the same son of the mountains that we thought he was. Not under these circumstances.

As time drags on, a heavy realisation hits me. Nobody can predict the ways of nature. You could be a mountain man all your life—like Suhas Bhaiya, who has grown up in these treacherous ranges—you could be as confident as the sheep that prance over these rocky slopes. But one day,

Nature will beat you down. One day you will find yourself cowering in a small tent, caught in the middle of Nature's wrath, hanging on for dear life. That day you will see that the wind doesn't blow at your call. The clouds don't really move to your command. And the mountains, oh, what do I tell you about the mountains, for they don't move at all.

And then it won't matter how much money you have. It won't matter how fit you are, or if you have run hundreds of miles. It won't matter if you are a marathoner training in the mountains. The treatment will be the same for everyone. And it will make you cry. Mark my words. It will make you cry like a helpless child as you gulp down the reality—along with the bile threatening to gush out of the mouth.

The tent is almost dark. Only the diffused light through the yellow plastic sheet tells me it is still daylight. It fills the tent with a dull yellow light that I have begun to associate with rain and sickness. Will we ever be able to get out of here? I wonder what time it is but am too weak to lift up my arm and look at the wrist watch. Besides, how does it matter? It wasn't like Suhas Bhaiya had told us the exact time the rain would stop, had he? And even if he had, again, how would it matter? He would only be wrong, just like every other time. I look around. I can't tell the time. It all feels the same. We have all been in the same position, since morning: Me lying down on the side, along the length of the tent wall. Kavyaa crouching next to me, to keep her head from touching the roof. And Suhas Bhaiya squatting at the opposite end of the tent next to the food supplies and the luggage.

The perpetual, deafening sound of the rain, the sporadic burst of thunder, the stinging silence inside the tent, and the occasional painful grumble in my stomach as the spasms pass: this isn't why I was in the Himalayas!

Suhas Bhaiya says that if we don't descend down the pass and reach the opposite foothill in three days, they will come looking for us with mules and food. Because they know we only have three days' supplies. Mules and food and medicines. Ah. Good Lord. But somehow they only seem like empty promises. They seem like a faint, far off world. A hazy, imaginary place. Because all that would happen only if the rain stopped. And what if it didn't stop? What if it went on for seven, eight, or even nine days? Then we would all die here in our watery grave. The thunder rumbles in the distance in agreement.

Inside the tent, Suhas Bhaiya is humming a song, probably with the intention of lifting our spirits, and his own. It doesn't help: His voice is barely audible. And the song he sings seems to have a melancholic note to it. I don't understand the words, but it sounds like something that a maiden would sing to her lover; a lover who never returns. If my intuitions are true, it is a ridiculous song to sing at such a time.

Kavyaa is doing things her own way to cheer me up. The last time she went out of the tent to attend to nature's call, she returned with some wildflowers: the same ones that we had seen, admired and photographed two days ago while on our way up; while the sun still shone. They were in different shapes, sizes and colours—pink with purple on long petals, yellow with red on round petals, white with black spots on heart-shaped petals. It gladdened the heart to find them growing wild, to see them emerging out of the smallest crack in the rocks. I casually happened to lean over the ledge and found an entire field of yellow and white wildflowers stretching unto the horizon. I was spell-bound! And in one wild second it made my life worth living. But that was two days ago.

***

Two days ago.

The sun is shining bright. The air is cold, and we are grateful for the warmth of the sun. Each time our trail takes us behind a huge cliff that blocks away the sun's rays, the cold breeze makes our teeth chatter, and we wait for the sun to find us again.

The path is extremely rocky. Suhas Bhaiya walks next to his mule, Raja, who is loaded with our luggage—a rolled-up tent, sacks of food supplies, a small stove and a can of kerosene. Raja, with his grey fur and long ears, seems to appreciate the occasional pats on his back that all three of us generously shower him with. In return, he nuzzles us with his cold, moist snout.

Suhas Bhaiya asks us who we think would be more expensive: a horse or a mule.

'Of course, a horse!' I exclaim. They are a lot bigger, and stronger, aren't they? Suhas Bhaiya guffaws like a horse. Perhaps like a mule. That ringing boyish laughter that turns his fair cheeks one shade redder. 'Wrong,' he says. 'A mule! A horse would never be able to climb so well,' he explains. 'Himalayan mules are known for their trekking expertise. I paid two lakhs for this boy!' he pats Raja on the back. Raja swings his tail a couple of times and moves his ears back and forth in agreement. He seems to like his master. And as I see, his master seems exceptionally fond of him.

'Oh, look!' Kavyaa suddenly exclaims. 'Look at the sky!'

I look up. And all at once, I find myself overcome by an overwhelming sense of …blue. From all the looking down and walking, I realise I had failed to notice the sky all this while. And now that the sun is high up, it is bluer than ever. It isn't an ordinary blue. No. Not even something that can be called a deep blue. It is a spectacular—an almost unbelievable—Himalayan blue. Blue that fills you with so much life you would think it would, in a strange way, make you immortal. All you want to do is gaze up and take in as much of the sky as you possibly can.

I run up the slope, careful to jump safely over loose rocks, and climb to the edge of a large rock or a small cliff with a view. There I wait, knocked out of breath, trying to breathe in the thin Himalayan air, as I wait for Kavyaa, Suhas Bhaiya, and Raja to catch up. And then I sprint further up ahead. Marathon training doesn't get better than this, I think to myself. I hope spending a few days running around in the thin high altitude air would make me a better runner when I go back home.

My reason for going trekking in the Himalayas was simple: I wanted to train to run at a higher altitude for a few days because it helps adapt the body to carry oxygen more efficiently. Once back at sea level, one can run better. When I had told Kavyaa about my plan, she had asked me in all earnestness: 'Will there be wildflowers? I will come along with you for the wildflowers.'

Feeling unsure, I had promised her there would be. Honestly, I had not understood the big deal about wildflowers. But maybe, on the other hand, she probably didn't understand the big deal about high altitude training. It shouldn't be difficult to find a few wildflowers, should it, I had thought.

And indeed, there was an unimaginable number of them, in so many hues that it was almost surreal to stand amidst them. At times, as I scurried up and waited, Kavyaa and Suhas Bhaiya would take too long to reach me, and I would know for certain that some pretty little flower would have probably caught Kavyaa's attention. And then, I would have to cup my hands and shout out to them, and hear intently, waiting for the breeze to bring back their reply. If it didn't come, I would scramble down again to catch them midway. A tiny violet flower would have found its way behind Kavyaa's ear.

'How do you do it?' Kavyaa had asked, intrigued by the number of times I ran up and down. The lack of oxygen had her panting. A light sweat had formed on her brow despite the chill in the breeze. Her face was turning pink.

'You just have to be strong,' I had told her. 'If you believe you can keep going, you really can!' I had set off again, disappearing behind a large boulder in ten seconds.

I stop to admire the view. It is a steep fall, probably 2,000 feet. I glance behind me; Suhas Bhaiya, Raja and Kavyaa look like tiny specks in the landscape. I have to trace back my gaze along the trail to spot them. Like three small ants in colourful clothes, they clamber slowly towards me, their movement almost imperceptible. As if in a different world where time moves really slowly.

After a few hours, we decide to call it a day. I could have gone on longer, but Kavyaa is tired. She says she wants to spend some time by the stream that we have just reached. Sitting by the babbling waters, she wants to sing and sketch and cook by the bonfire. We help Suhas Bhaiya pitch our tent. Raja is set free to graze, much to his delight.

We sit on rocks and dip our feet in the cool spring until it begins to freeze our toes. Soon, the temperature drops drastically as the sun disappears behind the mountains. We miss the sunset because of a few clouds in the horizon. Suhas Bhaiya examines the sky and says we might face a wet night, but we don't pay much attention to his words. They are just a few grey clouds; what harm could they possibly cause.

Lighting a small fire from the dry twigs that Suhas Bhaiya has collected, we sit around it and gobble up the vegetable porridge. As Kavyaa begins to sing, the universe seems to fall silent. Her melodious voice fills the silent chasm in the mountains, and suddenly, they feel complete. Even Raja comes by and settles next to the fire, chomping on the vegetable peels that his master has thrown him.

Sitting opposite me, her face illuminated orange by the fire, Kavyaa looks like the most beautiful woman in the world. Her eyes are shut as she sings, and her face is glowing. She seems to be in her own world. I wonder what kind of a world it would be inside that head. One thing I know for certain. It would have wildflowers. Yes. Lots and lots of wildflowers.

I smile dreamily into the fire. The warmth from the flames and the sound of the music is so moving, it makes me wish the song, the fire, and the night would last forever.

It doesn't. But when the song does end, nobody says a word. Somehow, even a tiny word of appreciation seems too intruding. For the pristine fabric that Kavyaa has created with her music hangs in the night, like a soulful spell. We sit under the mesmerising galaxy of stars, silently vanquished by the incantation. It was a song I had never heard her sing before. A song sung by a small girl waiting for the rain to shower down over her, and fill up the stream, so it could carry her paper boat away. The little girl looks skywards and prays to the clouds. She asks if prayers are ever answered. And then, the song ends. It leaves behind an almost heart-breaking rift in the mountains. A cruel abyss.

For a long time, only the crackling of the fire, and Raja's occasional snorting, is audible. And then the little girl's prayers are answered.

The first few drops of rain begin to fall upon us.

***

Inside the dingy tent, the fever comes up like an uninvited guest; like a traitor slowly creeping in. I feel my body heat up as the fever begins to set in. My thermals are soaked in sweat. Kavyaa dabs away at my forehead with a piece of cloth that has been made damp with the chilling rain water from outside. I don't know if it is helping.

That, however, is not the best thing Kavyaa is doing. The best thing is that she is keeping her cool. At a time when I think I will not make it to the next hour, she is amazingly strong. That makes me feel a lot better. Probably because it fills me with a fake sense that maybe I am not as sick as I feel. And maybe I won't die.

'You are strong,' she keeps telling me, but I feel otherwise. She gives my hand a little squeeze. With the slight bit of energy that I have, I respond back with a much gentler squeeze. It could be Kavyaa's way of making sure I am still alive. And I must respond back. Kavyaa has asked me to keep the hopes high. And I must not give away any sign that I am sinking.

'Remember what you told me the other day?' Kavyaa tries to talk to me. Her voice sounds distant. As if she is somewhere far away. Why is she so far away? What other day is she talking about? Let me see. Today is... What day is it today? When did we leave? It seems quite a task trying to recollect things. They seem so long ago. As if they are simply memories from childhood. Faint and vague. But happy and sunny. I give up trying to think. All that keeps playing in my mind is hours and hours of rain. Maybe it isn't just me. Maybe everyone in the tent has lost track of time. Or the day. Or the date.

So what was Kavyaa saying? She is peering into my face now. Is she asking me to remember things? I want to tell her I can't. But I don't have the strength to. I just want to sleep. But Kavyaa goes on. She is asking me to be strong. 'Remember what you said? If you can believe you will make it, you will! As long as you believe that you will pull through, nothing can pull you down.'

Suhas Bhaiya has stopped singing now. There is a silent look of worry on his face. After a while he gets up to leave. He says he will try reaching the village somehow to get some medicines. We watch as he puts on his black rain jacket, and then pulls the hood low over his eyes. Head bent and hands in his pockets, he goes out into the storm.

Lifting the flap just a few inches, Kavyaa observes as his brawny figure keeps going further away from the tent, until the heavy blanket of the rain engulfs him. 'Take care,' she whispers to him, as if he is right next to her. We wonder how he will cross the stream. Didn't he say it will be impossible? Well, he is a man of the mountains; he will know what to do. She observes the rain for a few more seconds as if half expecting Suhas Bhaiya to return immediately. Then with a sigh, she shuts the flap of the tent and turns back to me.

Just then, a deafening explosion goes off in the distance.

'What was that?' Kavyaa sits up, her eyes wide.

I don't know. I don't want to know. If it was meant to kill us, then so be it. I am going to die anyway. The second explosion, louder this time, is much closer. Visibly shaken, Kavyaa lifts open the flap of the tent and peeps out. From the mountain range opposite us, massive boulders are tumbling down in free fall. After falling for over a thousand feet, they crash and explode like grenades.

In all my life so far, it is the most frightening sight I have ever seen: the wrath of the Himalayas. The horrifying vehemence of the mountains unfurling before our eyes. What makes it more frightening is the fact that it could very well happen on our side of the mountain range too. In that case, the tent—and our lives—would merely be a castle of cards in the wind.

'What do we do now?' Kavyaa asks, as if I have an answer. 'What if it takes down Suhas Bhaiya?'

I had never thought of that. One tiny rock could hit you like a bullet. And these were hundreds of them, a hundred times bigger! I realise that if he doesn't return, we will never find our way back from here.

'I wish Suhas Bhaiya was here!' Kavyaa's voice sounds shaky, but somehow she manages to hold back tears. I don't know how that would help; Suhas Bhaiya wouldn't have been able to stop the rock fall. Or even the rain, like we had seen. But I can't deny the fact that his presence would have felt a lot calming. The tent would have felt a lot safer. Not knowing what to do, we remain in silence, listening to the frequent rock explosions outside the tent. It seems to be getting dark. The yellow from the tent roof isn't so bright anymore. Or is it the clouds? Or is it just my eyes?

'I don't want to die,' I whisper, almost breaking down. The pain is exhausting, and I am crumbling. I am not even a shadow of who I was two days ago, jumping over rocks, climbing up and down the trail.

'You are not going to die,' Kavyaa assures me, clutching my arm tight, as if that will keep me from dying.

'But I hardly feel any better. What if I don't get better? What if I...' I give up. Talking is taking up too much energy.

'Look, if you think you are not getting better, you never will. You know what? You are not being strong!'

What! Did she just accuse me of not being strong? Did she not see me run up the slopes the other day? I am strong. Right now, I am just sick. But I am too weak to argue. With my eyes shut, I merely listen.

'Anybody can be strong when everything is fine,' she says. Her gaze is perennially fixed to my face every time I open my eyes. 'But when everything in the world is upside down, and yet you remain strong, that is when you are truly strong!' I remain silent. She does sound right.

'It is no big deal to bloom when the sun is shining,' Kavyaa continues. 'But it takes a goddamned wildflower to bloom when it is raining havoc!' With this, she falls silent. She is holding a small bouquet of the wildflowers that she had collected earlier in the day. Placing it in my palm, she curls my fingers around it. Despite the darkness, and the tempest roaring outside, the little flowers seem to be smiling back at me with assurance.

'I don't need to tell you this; I am sure you know it already. When you run a race...' she stops.

My eyes flick wide open. The words grab my attention.

'In a race, anybody can run the first kilometre. What decides the winner is how strongly you run the final kilometre, isn't it? What matters is how well you run when the body is giving up, when you are in extreme pain, when all you want to do is quit. That is when you have to be mentally strong, don't you think? Physical strength will only get you where it gets everyone. But to win the race, you must believe you are strong, even when...' she stops again, as if unsure about finishing it. Then she says it. In a hushed voice, and yet with astounding firmness: '...Even when you are dying.'

I don't know if it is from the cold, or from the way she speaks, but it gives me goosebumps. Of course, it is nothing new. There was no rocket science or words of philosophy there. But the simple idea somehow strikes me like a bolt from the heavens. Like a split second of illumination. It has never made as much sense to me as it does in this desperate moment where I hang on to my dear life.

In this tiny yellow tent, in the middle of the furious Himalayas, stuck in a never-ending storm, and listening to the howling winds, the pattering rain, and the exploding rocks, I suddenly seem to have discovered the secret ingredient I had been looking for. Of course, it would take me years to practice and master what I had learnt. It would take patience and mental training before I can begin to win races. But if you were consumed by a sickness that made you feel you wouldn't make it past a few hours, and suddenly you chance upon something that makes you want to think about tomorrow, you would come to believe that you have found the elixir of life. And the utter simplicity of your new found treasure makes you laugh, but it is in these simple colours that life's meticulous mysteries are painted, aren't they?

Kavyaa is observing me silently. She doesn't say more; she doesn't need to. If her words were inspiring, the ensuing silence is electric. It speaks to me louder than the torrential rain over the roof; louder than the storm hurling the boulders. When the going gets tough, Kavyaa seems to say... That is when the wildflowers get growing!

For the first time in thirty-five hours, I find the strength to look up at Kavyaa and smile.

***

Darkness envelopes the tent once again. We sing a small prayer together. Or rather, Kavyaa sings, and I move my lips in sync. We both know without expressing it that it is a prayer for Suhas Bhaiya; a prayer to keep him safe from any harm.

The wait is dreadfully long. And with every passing minute, with every explosion of the rocks, his return becomes more and more uncertain. I find myself drifting into sleep. But Kavyaa remains awake and alert to the faintest sounds outside the tent.

It is still dark when we hear footsteps. Heavy, slushy footsteps.

'Hear that…?' Kavyaa hisses in alarm. I snap my eyes open.

The tent flap opens and in comes Suhas Bhaiya. A wave of relief washes over us. Kavyaa hugs him and begins to weep out of happiness. I manage to raise half an arm, and greet him with a faint, hoarse wheeze. He is drenched to his bones and his sorry face tells us that he has returned empty-handed. But to us, the fact that he has returned is far more relieving than any medicine he could have brought back.

'The stream...' he apologises. 'It was impossible to cross the stream.'

'It is okay,' Kavyaa consoles him. 'He is better. He even ate some oats,' she lies to reassure him. Then she asks, 'How did you escape the shooting rocks?'

'I don't know,' he sighs, visibly relieved. 'It didn't happen where I was. Not a pebble hit me. It was as if someone was praying for me.'

Kavyaa glances at me and smiles. In the dim candlelight, I see her cheeks are streaked with tears.

Maybe it was our prayer that worked. Or maybe, Suhas Bhaiya believed with all his heart that he would get back safe. Maybe when the storm was raging over him, he decided he was stronger than the night. Perhaps when it was raining rocks, he decided he was... a Himalayan wildflower.

Instead of medicines, Suhas Bhaiya does bring along a change in weather. The rain reduces to a drizzle, which is only audible if everybody in the tent remains silent. The rocks cease to fall. And the wind dies down. And as I stumble out of the tent to dump out the imaginary oats that I have ingested, for the first time in over forty hours I need a toilet paper roll to wipe my behind clean.

***

Three hours later, when we wake up, we open the tent flap to the most beautiful Himalayan morning we have ever seen. The storm has passed and all that remains is blissful sunshine. The bowl of yoghurt that I ate the previous night, and managed to retain, seems to have done me some good. I feel much better than yesterday.

Having pulled me through the night, having remained strong through the darkest hours, Kavyaa finally seems to run out of strength. She looks at the sunshine, and breaks down, weeping hysterically. She cries like a baby, holding her bouquet of wildflowers close to her chest. It makes my eyes moist to look at her happiness. I hug her and for one wordlessly beautiful moment we cry in each other's arms. We both know, together we have made it through the worst.

Raja is grazing on fresh grass in the warm sunlight as if he has always been there. Suhas Bhaiya, too, is sitting in the sun, boiling tea in a kettle. The golden rays pass through the steam from the kettle, and stream into the tent through the open flap. I laugh as Kavyaa runs out to collect some more wildflowers.

Will there be wildflowers? I will come along with you for the wildflowers, she had told me.

Wildflowers. That was why she was in the mountains. Clambering over rocks. Trudging over slopes. Braving stormy nights. Handing me toilet paper rolls from the tent. All for these wildflowers. It hadn't made sense to me back then. Why should wildflowers be so important to her, I had wondered. But I get it now. Perhaps, after all, wildflowers are all there is to life. And maybe, in this ironically strange way, I, too, was here to collect wildflowers.

I had come to the mountains hoping to get some strength in my lungs and in my legs. But I found myself barely able to sit up. I had hoped to discover some complex ingredient that would make me a better marathon runner. And I realise the mountains handed me the simplest truth there ever was, to make me a better person. I had trekked all the way here, hoping to collect some priceless memories. And in return, the storm threw rocks at me, and had me hanging on for life. And all I collected were lessons. Lessons from wildflowers.

And as for Kavyaa, she was here for the wildflowers, and with the wildflowers she would return.

She comes back to the tent, a little skip perceptible in her gait, humming a tune to herself. There is a smile glued to her lips. There is sunshine on her face. There is a twinkle in her eyes. And a bunch of Himalayan wildflowers in her hair.

Maybe, if I really learned from them, the wildflowers would teach me how to become a stronger runner. Maybe they could teach me how to win races.

Or maybe, they would merely teach me how to bloom like them somewhere in the middle of the tall, furious mountains, on a cold, dark, stormy night, outside the small yellow tent of three lonely travellers with a mule.

As I venture out of the tent to stretch my legs in the sun, I notice something that fills my heart with warmth, and makes me smile. Just outside the tent, under the open flap, and dancing merrily in the sun, four of the most breathtakingly beautiful Himalayan wildflowers have grown out of the damp grass.

'Who is the fourth one for?' Kavyaa asks.

'It is for Raja,' Suhas Bhaiya smiles, and the mule moves his ears back and forth in happiness.

***

gone

Every time I head out for a run, the early morning stillness on the farm is invariably shattered by Bruno's volley of barks. A half-Labrador, he is the happiest dog you will ever meet. As I step out of the farm gate, he jumps and clings onto me with his front paws, while his wagging tail rings against the metal gate, trying to convince me to take him along. What follows is a display of the tricks I have taught him since he was a puppy—high-fives, roll-overs, spot jumps—to persuade me that he is indeed qualified to accompany me for my run.

I sometimes do take him along. When running in loops, I have him guard my bottle. But no, I can't have him run along with me. He always ruins my pace because all he wants to do is chase birds and rabbits along the way. And so, I leave him behind, chained to the gate.

***

The sun is just about to break out of the golden horizon as I start off at an easy pace. The summer breeze feels warm against my face. The pungent smell of mango blossoms lingers heavily in the air. Far away, I can still hear Bruno's barks and howls cutting across the sleeping countryside and its silent trees.

I wish he would shut up. It makes me feel guilty to leave him behind. Each bark tells me a story of hope. Very much like every single race that I have run in the past one year, and have tried to break thirty-five minutes for ten kilometres—and failed. The last time I failed, I felt so hopeless, I decided I would never make it. That was two days ago.

But Bruno exudes the same hope morning after each morning: that I will take him along this time for sure. His black gleaming eyes are always filled with undiminished enthusiasm, his actions never blemished by the previous morning's disappointment. And that tail continues to wag against the gate with unmitigated passion, only to witness the gate being shut on his face again. But each morning he starts afresh, with no ill feelings, and no love lost. Hope unsullied. Barking with the same belief for something he knows might never happen.

I feel a sudden catch in my throat. If only I believed in myself even half as much as Bruno does in his barks...

***

One afternoon, I am driving back home when my mother calls. Her tone tells me something is terribly wrong. Her voice is cracking, and she is gasping. Then the words spill out of her mouth all at once. 'Call up the vet! Quick!' she shrieks. 'Bruno has been stung by honey bees!'

WHAT!

'He tried to bite a honey comb in the bushes, and got attacked!'

Without glancing into the rear-view mirror, I pull over rashly to the side. In a haze of confusion, I call up the vet.

'You will have to get him to the hospital as soon as possible. Earlier the better,' the doctor tells me. His voice is surprisingly calm.

'But we live thirty kilometres away, in Umarsadi!' I panic.

'There is no other way! If there is someone who knows how to inject a shot, get Avil anti-venom shots from the pharmacy.'

'What shots?'

'A-V-I-L!'

I hang up. I am in the middle of the highway. Cars and trucks zoom by barely two feet away from the side of the door. The engine of the pick-up is still running. My hands are shivering and there is a terrible wrench in my gut as if someone is squeezing out my insides. I am unable to think. I have no idea what to do. The closest pharmacy is in the marketplace, crowded with people and vehicles. How do I get there with this farm pick-up?

I pull over and get out of the car. I don't even know if it is legal to park where I leave the pick-up, on the side of the highway. I don't remember locking the vehicle. In a flash I am sprinting to the marketplace, weaving through a mass of honking cars and overflowing people. The mess we call humanity. I run all the way to the pharmacy, repeating A-V-I-L over and over in my head.

A syringe. A needle. One Avil shot. A-V-I-L. No carry bag. Thank you.

I smash down fifty bucks on the counter, for what was probably worth twenty, and start sprinting back to the pick-up. My head is crowded with thoughts. All I know is I need to get Bruno to the vet.

Earlier the better, the vet had said. I sprint harder until I get back to the vehicle, thoroughly spent. My legs are trembling so hard it is impossible to press the clutch down. Somehow I manage to get home.

And then I see him. Bruno is lying on his side, panting hard, froth forming in his mouth. My mother is desperately splashing water over his face.

I can't take it. 'BRUNO!' A heart-wrenching scream escapes my mouth as I fall on the ground next to him. His eyes are open, and he tries to lift his head when he hears me, but fails.

I have never seen him like this before. Unable to digest it all, I break down.

'The vet said we need to inject this. And we need to get him to the hospital!' I tell my mother, my voice loaded with panic and helplessness. Tears start streaming down my face. 'He will be fine,' my mother tells me, but her voice conveys just the opposite.

I have never injected a shot to anyone before. My mother hasn't, either. Should I try? What if something goes wrong! But what if it goes right! What a dilemma!

I look at Bruno. He is panting frighteningly harder now. His mouth is foaming much more than before. Through his half-shut eyes, I see my own life flashing before me.

I decide to take a chance. I fix the needle, pierce the bottle, suck in the liquid. All I know is that no air bubble should remain in the syringe. I clean the area with spirit, like I have seen doctors do. My hands are trembling and I am a nervous wreck. I can feel my heartbeat against the plastic body of the syringe. With a deep breath, I lower the needle to his body, almost touching his fur. And then I stop dead.

No! I can't do this! I just can't...

My mother urges me on. I hold my breath as if the needle is piercing into my body. It pricks me like I am the one getting the shot. I wince in pain as I empty the contents of the syringe and pull the needle out. And I hope that it works.

Next, we haul Bruno up in the back of the car. I get in with him. My mother takes the wheel. *Bruno! Bruno! I've got you, strong boy! You're going to be fine!* I keep telling Bruno through the tears. 'His breathing is slowing down, Maa!' In response, I hear my mother press down the accelerator a little more. The engine roars.

You've got to make it, Bruno! I shake him desperately, trying to get him to his senses. He opens his eyes, wearily, only to shut them again. Tears run down my cheeks, landing on Bruno, forming crisp round droplets on his fur. Just like how he gets dew on his coat when playing in the garden. It makes me want to hug him tighter and cry harder.

Bruno! Please, Bruno! We are almost there!

But Bruno is sinking. His breathing is dangerously slow now. And I can barely feel his pulse. 'Maa...!'

There is nothing she can do. She is already doing a hundred and twenty kilometres an hour on the highway.

I try pumping his chest with my palms. *BRUNO!* I yell close to his ears, bending over and clutching him tight in my arms. He doesn't open his eyes this time, but what he does shatters my heart into a million pieces. Worn out and spent as he is, he gives his tail a little wag against my chest. As if saying a final goodbye. As if telling me he was happy I was by his side.

In all these years of my life, there has been nothing that has moved me as much as this one single moment; that one single tail wag.

And that is it. A final sharp breath escapes his mouth. And then silence.

He is gone; it is all over.

For the first time that evening, my mother breaks down. In the rear-view mirror, I see her cover her mouth with her palm and let the tears flow. They flow profusely with the breeze that blows in through the rolled-down windows of the pick-up.

We bring Bruno back to the farm. There, under the very mango trees he chased rabbits around, we lay him to rest. He looks so much at peace, as if he is simply sleeping. Happy. Resting in his own little place he called home. Surrounded by the people who meant the world to him. A free soul now. Free to run when he wants to. Free to chase birds and sniff into burrows. No gate, however strong, could hold him back anymore.

The soft, late evening sun casts long, faint shadows on the ground. The smell of mango blossoms fills my nostrils again. The air is still; a little too still for comfort. I lower myself to my knees and shut my eyes tight. Head bent low, I muster a small, silent prayer for Bruno.

***

I don't know how much time I spend there by his grave, lost in a deluge of emotions. When I open my eyes, the darkness of the dusk has begun to surround me. The sun has long set. Even though it is a little too late to go for a run, I need it. I need to be by myself. Apprehensively, I put on my shoes and walk towards the gate.

The gate.

My heart begins to race. This is going to be the toughest part. I try to distract myself and hurry out, but it seems impossible. The gate feels dreadfully desolate. Unfriendly. Silent. No barks. No tail wags. No jumps. The calm is devastating. The silence is deafening. I can't take the stillness anymore. I break into a run. Even as I try to resist it, my ears strain to listen to barks in the distance. Nothing. Only the hollow sound of the wind in my ears as I run.

I speed up, listening intently. Still no barks. I am running at a pace I know I wouldn't be able to sustain beyond a few hundred metres. But I want to keep going. Somehow, I *need* to keep going. I need to get it all out of me. Every single memory. Every bit of energy. Every ounce of life. I need to run away from that gate. And yet, towards the barks. The barks that I will never hear again. It is all so cruelly ironical! The irony makes me want to throw up. The running makes me want to puke.

And then I let it all go. Bending over with hands on my knees, I let loose the emotions I had held back for what seemed like an eternity, and let it all out. The guilt, the love, the regret, the pain, the isolation. And more than anything, Bruno's final tail wag. They all show up together, surrounding me, stripping me naked, beating me down mercilessly. And I break down yet again. Like a child. Shamelessly. In the very middle of the road. In full view of the world around me. Hidden by nothing but the looming veil of dusk.

It is funny how I walked out of that gate every single day, invincible and unyielding, until the sheer distance I ran, silenced Bruno's barks. And today I am this emotionally fragile, psychologically vulnerable being who can't even run beyond the first kilometre. I feel shattered from within. The emptiness in me is disastrously overwhelming. I wish I had taken him out for a run sometime. I wish he hadn't wagged his tail just before he breathed his last. I wish...

There are so many wishes. Wishes that will simply remain wishes. Unfulfilled. Broken. Time will not turn itself around. I want to hug him. I want to run with him. There is so much left to do. But he is gone.

***

Bruno wasn't just a pet dog. He was family. He was this amazing creature with soft muddy paws, gleaming black eyes and a perennially wagging tail who taught me hope. He taught me how to believe in my efforts. Morning after morning at the gate, with his hopeful barks and expectant eyes, he taught me perseverance. And how never to give up.

I often think about my goals standing tall before me. After all, in life we are all a little too hopeful, aren't we? Or dare I call us hopelessly optimistic? Utopian fantasists, perhaps? For we chase dreams we might never get to all our lives. We hope to reach places far beyond our reach. But in the end, perhaps all that matters is how true our hope was. And how passionately we believed in our dreams.

In the end, it is all about whether or not that beautiful hope—that far-fetched dream—could put a smile in your black, sparkling dog-eyes, and a wag in your brown, furry, Labrador tail. And if you got that much, I think you won the battle already.

Bruno was probably an angel in disguise who had come to teach me some simple yet indispensable life lessons, and disappeared into thin air when I had learnt them. And as he went away, if there is one lesson I would never forget all my life, it is this:

He taught me what a beautiful place the world would be, if we could, but for a moment, treat the people around us like they were—gone...

The hollow sound of my footsteps and the daunting stillness at the gate as I run out every morning serve as a perpetual reminder.

***

dhanyavaad!

Silence. The city of Meerut is engulfed by the veil of silence. Silence, except for the sound of my shoes striking the hard pavement.

This is rather uncommon for this little north Indian city, whose bustling by-lanes are usually clogged with people who for some reason are always rushing about and yet finding time to have a quick snack of bread pakoda. Amidst honking autorickshaws, impatient heads attached to craning necks emerge out of crawling vehicles every now and then in an attempt to discern how much further the traffic trail stretches. However, today there is silence. And the city is asleep.

Yesterday was Diwali, the festival of lights. The beguiling lights and colours of the firecrackers had kept those out on the terraces awake all night. The deafening sounds had meted out the same treatment to those in their beds. But today the city is asleep except for sporadic explosions of crackers far away in the distance that still continue to enthral a handful of youngsters. And the occasional and faint clanking of the temple bells nearby that amuse the grey-haired and bent-over oldies. Those unobtrusive sounds keep me company as I run. During the intervening periods of silence, I listen to my footsteps and watch my shadow shorten and disappear as I pass under a lamppost, only to stretch and elongate in a matter of seconds until I get to the next one. Dawn seems to have decided to sleep in, too. But in the early morning darkness, apart from the few dimly-flickering patches that appear intermittently along the road, the tall lampposts cast a perfect golden glow over the empty, forlorn streets.

Bits of paper. The streets are covered in shreds of white and red paper. Worthless, mundane remains of the once magnificent crackers that had set the previous night's sky on fire. They cover the ground, each tiny bit trying to evade me, magically moving away just as my foot is about to land on them.

The air is still heavy with the lingering haze and smoke. It hangs like a translucent curtain before my eyes, making it difficult to breathe. The air is cold, and it makes the smoke feel terribly dense and still. So still, as if keeping up with the sleeping streets and the morning silence. I can taste the sulphur in the air with every breath. As a child, I always wondered how suffocated the trees must feel. I still do.

Nothing about the smoke surrounding me suggests cheer. And yet the air smells festive; it is the fragrance of sweets and holidays, of glittering oil lamps. I often wonder what it is about Diwali that makes one feel such warmth. Is it because everybody is with their families and surrounded by the people they love? Could it be because of the strings of colourful lights in every house? The temple bells and the sweets? Or because of how well they clean the streets? Maybe also because everybody seems to make extra money during Diwali—from beggars to businessmen. I don't know where the money flows in from. But somehow it does. Somehow God is kind. And somehow everybody is happy.

The glittering lights and the play of my shadow keep me entertained throughout the run. Back home in the countryside, you don't find such lights. Nor such little delights. You don't get to run under this yellow glow of streetlamps, for there aren't any. There are only golden sunrises and sanguine sunsets. And before the break of dawn, there are only sleepy cows and defecating farmers staring blankly at you through the darkness as you go running by.

***

An hour later, tired and hungry, and perspiring profusely, I make my way back. The sun is almost up, but behind the cloak of dense smoke, it looks like a hazy white ball that resembles a full moon. Like the firecrackers have stolen all its fire and now it only hangs shamefully, cold and naked. The city seems to be coming to life, although reluctantly. The sky is brightening, and the yellow street lights have given way to blinking signal lights. The pigeons have begun their deep, low-pitched chanting. This is the sound I always associate mornings in the city with. For there are no pigeons on the farm; only the roosters, the faraway peacocks, and the distant barking of the village dogs. It is an interesting sight to see a city waking up. So many events happening all at once.

A sweet shop has opened its shutters, expecting to serve some early patrons. A pot-bellied man, his hairy torso covered in a plain white vest, stands next to a huge pot on a flame, stirring its contents like a wizard working on his magic potion. The thick smell of over-heated oil reaches my nostrils as I run by.

Pat. Pat. Pat. Pat. The feet strike the footpath in perfect rhythm, and the sound echoes against the closed shutters along the narrow alley. I realise how rare it is to hear footsteps while running in the noisy city on days other than Diwali. Pat. Pat. Pat. I land a bit harder, trying to make the most of the quiet streets. And then, as I turn into the adjacent lane, a new sound greets me at the corner.

Swish. Swish. Swish. Swish. A young chap, dressed in a brown uniform, is sweeping the pathway with a broom whose cane handle rises well above his own head.

I don't know if it is the Diwali in me, or the endorphins from the run, but I am overcome by a sense of gratitude. It is also the Gujarati new year today. I realise that while the city sleeps, this man must go about his job cleaning the streets.

I come to a halt; I don't want him to become aware of my presence. I am embarrassed at how privileged I am, and ashamed of how much I take that privilege for granted. From behind the lamppost in the corner, I observe quietly as he goes about his business, carefully directing the remains of the firecrackers towards a heap on the side, so it looks like Diwali when the city wakes up. So that the streets are clean when the people walk out. And all that for what? A few bucks to fill his tummy? All this for people he doesn't know at all? For people who will never acknowledge his efforts? He would have long departed by the time the people come out of their houses. Gone off with his tall broom to some other narrow alley. For he has many more streets to clean. He has an entire city to ready for the new year.

A deep sadness fills my heart. Doesn't he, too, deserve to be celebrating the festive season with his family? On any other morning, I would probably have run by. But today, I feel the need to walk up to him and thank him. My mother always says that if one shows gratitude on the first day of the new year, one is likely to have a great year ahead. Do one deed of kindness on new year's day for someone who will never be able to repay you, she would always say.

The day is brightening up, and the cooing of the pigeons has reached a crescendo. The sweeping of the streets has given way to a light, hazy curtain of dust hanging midway between the sweeper and me, almost separating his world from mine.

Shielding my nose from the dust, I take a few steps, a deep breath and break the dust screen, as I dive into his world. His dusty, hazy, lonely world.

Swish. Swish. Swish. He continues sweeping the streets even as he sees me standing next to him.

'Ram-Ram, Bhaiya,' I greet him.

'Ram-Ram!'

'Won't you take a holiday today?' I ask him in Hindi, trying hard to sound like a local.

He merely shakes his head. As if the green mask covering his mouth is keeping him from speaking.

'I wanted to thank you, Bhaiya,' I tell him. 'For cleaning the streets even on new year!' Just to make sure he understands, I add, 'Dhanyavaad!'

It should have ended there, and I should have been making my way home. I did not desire any further communication. But visibly warmed by my words of gratitude, he wants to shake hands with me. I accept his outstretched hand and give it a gentle shake.

'Dhanyavaad, Bhaiya!' he tells me from behind his mask. 'Nobody has ever said that to me before,' he says.

'Well, you should know how grateful everyone really is towards you. The city would be a filthy place without you cleaning it.'

'Really?' he asks, his voice cracking.

I nod solemnly. 'Alright, happy new year, then,' I tell him, making a slight move away.

'Same to you, Bhaiya!' he bows lightly.

'Aren't you going to be with your family today?' I ask curiously.

'My family doesn't live here. I live alone,' he replies. Then after a thought, as if impelled to say it, his eyes smile fondly, and he speaks again. 'Amma always sends me sweets that she makes at home. This year they haven't arrived yet,' he says, blinking back tears.

I awkwardly turn my gaze away to spare him the embarrassment. How could a few words of gratitude and a few simple memories move a toil-hardened man to tears?

I don't know what to say to him. I don't know when the sweets from his mother will reach him. So I simply pretend not to have heard him, and mutter a quick goodbye with a gentle pat on his back.

I keep thinking about him as I jog slowly away. As I turn the last bend and cross a sweet shop, I suddenly realise I could have bought the chap some sweets! Reluctant to go back, I brush away the thought.

Little do I know that a few months later, I will be compelled to buy him a box of sweets.

***

Silence. Again. A few months later, the entire city is engulfed by the veil of silence, yet again. Silence, except for the sound of my shoes striking the hard pavement.

And this time around, that sound proves too costly for me. I should never have stepped out at all. But how was I to know that running was a sign of disrespect!

Yesterday, a political leader passed away in the city. Today, they called for the entire city to remain shut. I wonder how that will bring him back from the dead. I wonder if Sahab would have permitted a curfew for any reason, had he been alive. It seems pointless to me.

Bits of paper. Yesterday, too, there were bits of paper everywhere. Yellow pamphlets. They covered the streets in a blanket, as if a flood had passed by, leaving behind a trail of yellow destruction. They lined the sidewalks, and hung in the bushes. They choked up the gutters, and flattened under passing cars. Uninvited, they entered the streets of the market until the shopkeepers swept them out. And until the paan-wallah collected them and hung them in a neat pile by the side of his seat, to be used as wrapping paper for the paan that his patrons would like to take away.

An old beggar picked up a discarded pamphlet and held it upside down. He couldn't read but he could sense the warning in it. He wondered what was happening to the city. He collected as many as he could, to be later sold to the paper recycling factory for a small sum that could buy him a piece of bread. Next to him, a hungry cow chewed on the yellow pamphlets from the garbage bin.

Somewhere in a narrow alley, a young sweeper dressed in a brown uniform picked up a pamphlet and read:

Important notice. The city will remain shut tomorrow to mourn the death of our beloved Sahab. By order.

It was an order: an order to mourn, even if you had nothing to do with Sahab.

The sweeper flicked it away with a look of indifference. It didn't change anything for him. He would still report to work at the same time tomorrow. Festivals and funerals were all the same to him.

People all around spoke in hushed whispers, as if their voices would disturb Sahab's departed soul. There was a feeling of fear in their tone. And then towards the evening, hundreds of burly, saffron-clad men went around the city, wreaking havoc and forcing the city to shut down. They left behind a procession of stones, splintered glass and pamphlets. Yellow pamphlets. Thousands of them.

And today, as the sun rises over the deadly silence, the pamphlets lie dead on the streets. Today, the same destructive men, dressed in white, pray for peace. I find it ironical as I run along the empty streets. May your soul rest in peace, Sahab, I whisper pitifully.

In a few hours, the crowds will occupy these streets to catch a final glimpse of Sahab on his way to his heavenly abode. Not an inch of space would remain. People on the footpath. People on the rail tracks. People leaning over from their balconies. People hanging from trees. People everywhere.

As of now, I am grateful the streets are empty. I like empty streets. Because more than running, they let me think freely. Maybe it is because I grew up in the countryside. And the countryside only has empty streets.

Pat. Pat. Pat. The sound of the feet echoes through the bleak emptiness of Meerut at the break of dawn. I jump over the flattened yellow pamphlets. Some of the papers continue to blow freely with the silent whiffs of the early morning breeze, from one street to the next. Sticking to my shins, until I manage to shake them off.

Even the pigeons seem to be unusually silent today. Why, I wonder to myself. Mornings in the city feel incomplete without the constant cooing of the pigeons. The streetlights are still lit up, much beyond the regular time. Still trying to burn bright against the rising sun that tries to overpower and extinguish them.

My feet carry me along hushed alleyways. Past the silent markets. Over the deserted flyovers. And only silence prevails. Like the city is dead. Like one night, the city slept and never woke up. And only a solitary runner remained.

And one sweeper.

Swish. Swish. In a nearby lane, not too far away from my pattering feet, his broom works in quick, firm strokes, sweeping away the yellow pamphlets to a heap in the corner. Even his sweeping is sensibly silent today.

But not my feet. All the while, the ceaseless pattering of my feet fills the streets. It rebounds against the metal shutters of the closed shops. It echoes through desolate parking spaces. It reaches the ears of the white-clothed, burly men with saffron bands around their heads.

And it makes their blood boil.

***

Eight men. I count eight men. In two groups of four. All dressed in white. Their saffron bands clearly visible on their brows, like a uniform mark of anger. If you fail to notice it on the saffron bands, you could see it in their eyes. Big, bloodshot eyes. Heavy eyebrows. And thick, fuming moustaches.

Who had dared to disobey their command? Who is that plucky guy in bright running clothes who had the audacity to disrespect their Sahab?

I hear a gruff shout, and it sends a shiver down my spine. Only two words: ‘Get him!’

I stand rooted to the pavement, over a sea of yellow pamphlets. Unable to react, my mind goes blank and my feet are numb due to hysteria. Should I run? Should I simply wait here and apologise? I didn’t mean any disrespect, I will tell them. I am sorry, I will tell them. I am a huge fan of Sahab, I will tell them. I will go back home this very instant. Of course they will understand. I throw a glance at the men running towards me.

No, they won’t.

Two hundred metres from the end of the street, they are sprinting towards me, waving canes over their heads, spitting fire, hurling abuse and brick rubble.

There is no stopping a group of angry men, my father has always told me. You never go against a mob. It doesn’t matter what they think individually. Collectively they believe even murder is a pardonable offence. And sometimes, for a mutually justifiable cause, it isn’t an offence at all.

One of the men throws a stone at me. It misses me by a couple of feet and goes flying past my legs.

Run, my brain tells me. Run! But my shivering legs don’t listen. Finally, I get it. I turn around and break into a mad sprint. The first thing I can think of is to disappear out of sight. I turn left into a narrow alley and soon the men follow me. Half a minute, and they will be in the very same lane as me again.

I run down the alley. An alarmed sweeper looks up from his work and moves to the side. He sees me in distress. And then he sees the men turning around the corner. He points to a parked car next to a heap of garbage at the far end. Without exchanging words, I understand he is asking me to hide there.

Under normal circumstances, I would have trusted my legs more than my ability to camouflage. But the streets are dangerously empty. And the company of even an unknown sweeper feels calming. And besides, for how long will I be able to outrun eight men!

Instantly, I dive behind the car and crouch behind the heap of yellow pamphlets, hoping desperately that the men don't spot me; that their yellow pamphlets keep me from their saffron fury.

Kicking up dust, huffing and puffing with fury, the eight men reach the spot. My heart is thudding against my ribs so hard, I feel I will explode. My rapid breathing seems deafening in the critical stillness. The more I try to suppress my panting, the more certain I feel that I am going to pass out. It is a dreadfully ghastly feeling.

'Where did he go?' One of the men shakes up the poor sweeper, and my heart skips a beat.

'What are you doing here?' demands the other.

Before the sweeper can respond, one of the men pushes him to the ground. A sting of wrath shoots through my head.

'I... I am cleaning the streets for Sahab,' I hear the sweeper plead. 'Please let me go, I am only doing a service for Sahab.'

It seems like a good enough explanation to the men. They let go of him.

'Where did he go?' they ask the sweeper again.

I can see their canes, the tips of which are visible from under the car. They look vicious and menacing. I find myself almost trying to hide behind the tyres, to avoid the canes from seeing me. The old car smells strongly of oil. Or grease. Yes, it is grease. To me, it smells of fear. And panic.

It is strange what the brain conjures up during times of crises. So dreadfully nervous I am trying to remain hidden, that for one desperate moment I consider emerging from my hiding place and apologising. Surrendering to the angry men. Better to reveal myself than let them search the place and spot me hiding. And suddenly, the next moment I think of creeping out and making a dash for the opposite end of the street. Thankfully, sense prevails, and I remain crouching with bated breath.

The screech of a motorbike tells me a couple of more angry men have arrived to join the first eight. 'Where did he go?' the men bellow, louder than ever, grabbing the poor sweeper by the collar.

Only ten metres. One car. And half a thousand pamphlets between us. My body feels paralysed. I stare at the ground. A yellow pamphlet stares back at me.

'He went straight,' I hear the sweeper stutter. 'I saw him take a left...' Then a pause.

For two entire panic-filled seconds, it seems as if they will catch his lie and start looking around the place for me. Behind the tree trunks. Under the cars. And there I would be. They are the longest two seconds of my life. But they seem to buy his story.

'If he is not there...' the men bark threateningly at the sweeper, 'we will come back for you!'

I watch with intense relief as the feet of the eight men begin to shuffle away, and the wheels of the motorbike disappear amidst a loud, dust filled roar. My head feels heavy. My chest stings. I realise I am still holding my breath. Slowly I breathe out for the first time in a long time.

I remain hidden behind the yellow pamphlets, still too scared to emerge. Too scared to face anything. Behind the pamphlets is my safe place. I wait. I hear footsteps again. And then the face of the sweeper peers at me from the other side of the car. A green mask covers half his face. His brown uniform is crumpled at the collar, where the men grabbed him.

'Get out, quick!' he says, with a note of urgency.

There is no time to thank him; no time for showing gratitude. The men could return any minute. Hurriedly, I follow him out of the lane, creeping behind parked cars.

That is the first time I notice something that seems to light a bulb in my head. The young sweeper is so short, the end of his broom rises above his head. I have seen him somewhere, haven't I?

Diwali! Yes, he is the same guy, isn't he?

'Bhaiya?' I whisper.

He turns around. Is it him? No, I could not tell. With that mask on, all sweepers look alike. I still take a chance. 'Do you know me?'

I see him smile behind his green mask. 'You can forget me, but I will never forget you, Bhaiya,' he says. 'You made my day on new year's!'

***

I sit outside the sweeper's one-room house, facing the railway tracks. After two hours, the city police finally manage to reach an agreement with the burly men. They come to a compromise: Sahab can't be brought back to life, but a statue of his shall be erected in the next two months. The strike is called off; the city heaves a sigh of relief. Under the pretext of wanting to see Sahab one last time, people turn to the streets, as if silently celebrating freedom. Engulfed in yellow flames, as Sahab celebrates his liberation from his worldly body, a city celebrates its liberation from the saffron-clad men. From the orders of the yellow pamphlets.

Warily, I, too, make my way towards the broad street. All the while, I keep thinking of the sweeper. I wonder if he would have helped me if he hadn't known me; if it weren't for that one word of dhanyavaad a few months ago.

I remember what my mother always said. Good deeds on new year's day will bless you for the entire year. She was right. And in that case, imagine what a good deed every day could do to you!

An hour later, I am at the sweeper's door again, this time with a small box of sweets, also filled with my gratitude.

There is no doorbell. I knock at the door. And wait. Thirty seconds pass. No sound from inside. I knock again, harder this time. Still no response. And then I notice the shining brass lock hanging on the door. I sigh to myself. He has left. I look around to see if any of his neighbours are around. I find none. I wonder what to do. Finally, I scribble that one word in Hindi. That is all I can think of. And in some strange way, it is all that makes sense in that moment. One small Hindi word on a large blank sheet of paper. Square in the centre.

Dhanyavaad.

Carefully, I place the paper under the little red box, and the box on the doorstep, just under the shining metal lock.

As I walk slowly away, I think of how powerful that one word must be. Dhanyavaad. That it could, in some unexplainable way, save my life today.

I look around the city as I walk back. I realise there are a hundred reasons to use that one word; a hundred reasons to feel grateful. All around the world, and in life, there will be angry saffron-clad men, I realise. But for every angry man, there exists one kind sweeper. There will be yellow pamphlets with cruel orders, but there will also be someone to sweep them all away the next day. For every kind word, there will be a kind deed in return.

For every dhanyavaad, there will be a life saved, just the way mine was.

Two policemen are standing in the corner with watchful eyes, surveying the goingons before them. I feel safe. With a smile, I walk up to them. 'Dhanyavaad, sir!' I say to them.

Somewhere not far away, outside the door of a one-room shanty facing the railway tracks, a young sweeper finds a small red box with a note at his doorstep.

'Dhanyavaad,' he reads from the piece of paper and smiles.

He opens the box and breathes in the aroma of the freshly prepared sweets. He keeps a little more than half of the contents for himself and shuts the box. Then, as an afterthought, he opens it again, picks out one more piece and stuffs it into his mouth. For two minutes he stands there, eyes shut, savouring every bit of the delicious sweet. Just like his mother's, he thinks! When he is done, he carefully replaces the lid, and carries the box away with him.

***

Two blocks away, an old beggar wakes up and lifts his head off a pillow of yellow pamphlets. He finds a small red box lying next to his aluminium begging bowl. He opens it to find freshly prepared sweets.

He looks skywards with a look of indebtedness, his palms pressed together. His eyes turn moist with gratitude. 'Dhanyavaad, Maalik!' he breathes.

Engulfed in a sooty haze, the silhouette of a young sweeper carrying a broom that is taller than himself is seen at the far end of the dusty street.

***

the left

'Whatever route you take, don't ever take that left after dark!' they warn me, as I go running by.

I roll my eyes, snickering under my breath. I have heard this story a dozen times since yesterday. It has been doing the rounds in this small village of Palsana that boasts of forests so dense that the dead silence inside almost roars in your ears like the sea that is eight kilometres away. There are rumours that the left leading into the woods is haunted.

I often take the route towards Palsana which is a little over ten kilometres from the farm. I like running along its quiet roads as they take me by the forest or through densely planted mango trees on both sides. Usually, I only hear the faraway vroom of a tractor working somewhere in the fields. And I only hear my footsteps. But now I hear strange stories, too.

Small villages with their benighted peasants are always abuzz with such tales. But I am neither a peasant nor a child anymore. I am not going to buy this story, I mutter to myself. Probably the only purpose these old wives' tales fulfil is to keep the village children from wandering too far from home. Maybe they also make for some interesting evening conversations. What else will a farmer talk to his neighbour about? That his paddy has grown one feet tall? And the neighbour replies that his cow gave six litres of milk today. And the next day? The paddy is still only one feet tall. And the cow still gives six litres of milk. Paddy and cows have pretty uneventful, insipid lives when it comes to that. Don't you need something interesting to discuss with your neighbour as you sip on tea and talk across the barbed wire fence?

And what better way—other than ghost stories—to spice up the day! The good part about them is that these stories need not be proven. Because nobody actually wants to *see* the proof! However burly their moustache may be. Or however hefty their cane. Talk about ghosts, and the moustache starts drooping. The cane starts to wobble. So you are at the liberty of your imagination, and you can take things as far as you let your creativity stretch. Or until the tea lasts. Whichever comes first. And you watch in silent glee as the neighbour's eyes go wide with horror, as he runs to tell his wife what you saw when you took a left into the woods last evening.

By the next day, you rub your palms out of delight and pat yourself on the back, as the entire village suddenly has something to talk about: The spirit residing in the woods. The ghost haunting the forest. Villagers, young and old, add their own flavourful descriptions and you can barely control your laughter when, the next morning, your story completes a full circle, and the neighbour from the other side comes over to tell you how he had heard stories about ghosts in the forest. And how you should avoid taking the left after dark.

It goes on until your own tale comes back to you so many times, and with so many spine-chilling variations, that you begin thinking of it as an ill omen, and really stop taking that left.

And when a young villager in running shoes goes sprinting by, you stop him and say, 'Whatever route you take, don't ever take that left after dark!'

***

In all likelihood, the origin of these ghost tales is as colourful as a young shepherd's vivid imagination. Maybe he has strayed too far with his herd of goats, looking for greener pastures. As the sun is setting, he begins to worry.

'Wow, just a little while ago, the sun was there,' the young lad tells Gori, his favourite goat, pointing his stick to the sky overhead. Gori bleats in response, as few perfectly round, black pellets of excreta fall out from under her tail, almost involuntarily.

The young boy is annoyed. 'You always have the same response for everything, don't you?' Gori bleats again. She is the most intelligent goat in the entire herd. And she is completely white. Not a fleck of black or brown on her, unlike the other goats. That is why she is called Gori.

It is getting dark, and the young lad needs to get back home with the herd. His father is not going to be too pleased. 'How many times do I have to tell you,' he will bellow. Anything that begins with that phrase has never done any good. 'You must act more responsible and get back home in time!' His father had rebuked him just the other day.

'He said he will confiscate my catapult if I get late again,' the boy complains to Gori. Gori nuzzles him with her snout and passes a few more pellets. What is the use of a catapult, anyway, she thinks.

The young boy gathers his goats, and urging them to move faster, guides them home. 'Haven't you eaten all day?' he chides them as they stop at every shrub. 'We need to get home before dark!' But the goats are stubborn and greedy. Before long, the sun sets. The boy starts to panic. He can't afford to lose his catapult. He looks at the left turn that runs through the woods. He will save at least fifteen minutes if he takes that route instead of going around the forest. The surprised goats bleat in confusion as their master makes a detour. But soon, they begin to follow. That is the good part about goats that makes them better than humans: they don't think too much.

It is pitch dark inside the forest. The canopy overhead is so thick that it takes a few seconds for the young shepherd to adjust to the darkness. For a moment, he wonders if he should turn back. But he doesn't want his goats to know that he is scared. They will never trust me again if I turn around now, he thinks to himself. And so, with hasty steps, he walks along. 'We should be home in twenty minutes, if you all hurry up,' he talks to his goats. He is not in a mood to talk so much, as much as he wants to retain his catapult. But the forest is lonely and terribly silent. He doesn't like the hollow sound of his footsteps echoing along the narrow winding trail. Talking to the goats makes him feel less frightened. 'This is not too bad a route, is it?' he asks Gori, in an effort to convince himself. This time, Gori doesn't bleat. She, like all the other goats, is silent. She, like the scared shepherd boy doesn't like the forest. She is used to grazing in open grasslands and going where she finds grass. Not where a narrow trail takes her. The forest, with its tall trees, makes her uneasy. What is the use of such tall trees anyway if even the tallest goat can't reach up to chomp on its leaves, she thinks to herself. Oh, maybe it is for birds to sit on. So that master can use his catapult on them. But if there were no trees, wouldn't the birds simply sit on the ground like normal goats? And then master wouldn't even need a catapult to catch them! Gori almost bleats away her bright suggestion out of excitement, but then holds herself back. I must remember this idea and tell it to master if his catapult gets confiscated. He will be so proud of me! A few pellets fall off her behind, from all the ardent thinking. She is, indeed, the most intelligent among the entire herd.

Walking next to her, the young master is getting worked up. What if they lose their way in the dark? They would have to wait until dawn for someone to find them! I would sure lose the catapult then, he thinks to himself, feeling a lot more alarmed.

A sharp pain shoots through the boy's foot. A massive thorn—the kind he has never before seen—is sticking into his flesh. Hastily, he pulls it out, making a mental note to watch out for more along the dark trail. 'This is what I don't like about the winters,' he talks aloud. 'For most part of the day, it is dark!'

Gori agrees. Shorter, darker days mean lesser time to wander. Suddenly, there is unrest among the herd. The goats are strangely still, as if listening to some inaudible sound. As a shepherd, the young boy knows exactly what this behaviour means. The shuffling. The pushing. It can mean just one thing. Wolf!

Goats can sense a wolf's presence long before the master can spot it. The boy becomes alert. Clutching his cane like a sword, he braces himself for the attack, like his father has taught him to. But his herd is large, and he starts feeling doubtful about being able to protect them all. He keeps Gori by his side. Nothing must happen to her. And sure enough, out of the dark, a giant of a wolf leaps out from behind the trees, landing right in the middle of the herd. All the goats scatter around the place, turning the quiet forest into a loud, bleating carnival. The boy hardly has time to react—and bring his cane cracking down—when the wolf grabs hold of one of the goats and disappears behind the trees, just as quickly as it had appeared.

The boy simply stands there, startled, too horrified to move. What will he say to his father about the missing goat? Why was there one goat less in the herd? He will surely lose his catapult now. He does not understand what the big deal should be, about a single missing goat. How does it matter if there are fifty-one or fifty-two? They still look like the same flock, don't they? Wait for a week and some goat would give birth to a kid. Wait for a month, and the kid would be big enough to graze with the herd. Why, then they would be fifty-two again! Yet he is relieved that his Gori is safe. He has a special bond with her. She is his favourite goat.

'What about my catapult?' the boy asks Gori. 'What do I tell father?' Gori does not reply. She is still scared. She has forgotten her bright idea out of fear.

The boy's eyes suddenly light up. He has an idea! Before the hungry wolf finds that one goat is too little for its supper and returns for another, the boy hurries with his goats out of the forest. Just as he is about to reach home, he starts crying at the top of his voice. 'Ghost! Ghost!' he shouts. His father comes rushing out with his cane.

'A hooded figure took away one of our goats!' the boy cries, his face white, and his eyes brimming with crocodile tears.

'Who? Where?'

'I was coming back home when a figure in a black robe appeared out of nowhere, picked up one of the goats and disappeared into the forest!' the boy wails. 'I gave a chase, but the ghost was too fast. It didn't even run, it floated above the ground. I ran into the bushes, look... Look at all these scratches, Baba...' the boy displays his arms that bear raw scratches from the thorny shrubs flanking the narrow forest trail.

'Oh, my poor boy,' the mother hugs the young shepherd. 'Don't ever take that left again!' she tells him, stroking his hair gently. The boy wails a little more until he is sure his catapult is safe. Then, with a sly smile, disappears into the barn to check on the goats.

By the following morning, the story has spread like wild fire. Soon, the entire neighbourhood knows how Chaitu

Babu's son lost a goat to a ghost. Everyone is talking about just one thing: the spirit haunting the woods. The milkman on the bicycle, the newspaper boy, and Parsot, the bullock cart driver, spread the story faster than the wind can.

'Hot news, ghost in the village!' the newspaper boy bellows as he cycles down the lane. The newspapers are sold out before nine, even though they say nothing about the ghost in the village.

'He had the hands of a skeleton figure. No skin, no flesh. Just bones!' Parsot tells a group of terrified farmers.

'They say you won't see him at first. You will only feel his presence. You will hear him breathing into your ears,' says the grocer to the tea shop owner, as he hands him his day's supply of groceries. The tea shop owner places his kettle on the stove to boil. Then, when the first customer arrives, he narrates the story about the ghost. 'You can hear his breath. And before you know it, you will be possessed, and follow him deep into the woods. There, he finishes you off. That is how he took the goat away. They even found the bones of the goat in the forest this morning. All snapped into two, broken, finished...' he shakes his head.

By the evening, the young shepherd has heard the story a dozen times already. Today he gathers his herd long before sunset, and starts making his way home. The stubborn goats want to stay a while longer, but the boy doesn't want to take any chances. He is scared stiff. He is going nowhere close to the woods. He is never taking that left.

Long before he reaches home, he starts believing his own story.

***

The first time the story comes to me, I burst out laughing. 'There is no such thing as ghosts,' I tell Parsot. 'They exist only in your imagination.'

Parsot is not happy to hear it. He doesn't understand imagination. He only understands bullocks. He shakes his head vigorously like his bullocks, and the jasmine oil in his hair fills my nostrils. 'Then prove it!' he says smiling mischievously.

'I will,' I tell him.

'One of these bullocks will be yours if you do,' he challenges me and turns around to leave. Was my description not eerie enough, he thinks to himself, as he drives his cart away. And how could all the villagers believe the story if ghosts really didn't exist?

The more versions of the story I hear, the more I am convinced that it is nothing but the villagers' imagination running wild. The poor, brainless peasants always believe in such tales. I must prove them wrong. I could win a bullock from Parsot. I must convince the villagers they are false stories. Before they end up convincing me that they are not!

Unlike in the cities, living in a small village, you can't escape darkness. It isn't the usual darkness, mind you! It is a strangely dense, impenetrable form of darkness. So black, you have to desperately blink a couple of times lest the surrounding vacuum pulls out the eyes from their sockets. Every nook and corner is dark after sunset. Every street, the open fields, and the mango orchards are dark as well. And the ghosts of your imagination surround you the moment you step into the darkness. Life is much easier when you don't believe in ghosts.

I make a mental plan to run through the dark forest at dawn and emerge on the other side along with the rising sun. The villagers will see with their own eyes that there is nothing to worry about. That there is no ghost. That they could go back to talking about their paddy and their cows. I will volunteer to make that happen. For I am not scared of ghosts. Nor am I scared of taking that left after it is dark.

***

The moon is high up in the sky, sailing alongside me, lighting up the road ahead, and enveloping the sleeping landscape in silver light. My breath makes tiny clouds of fog in the air. The cold January morning freezes my fingertips even though I have them tightly bound in a fist. The chill is getting into my head.

I reach the forbidden left that leads into the woods. There is nothing to contemplate; the decision has been made, and so I turn left. Fearlessly. As if it is the most natural thing in the world to do.

But then, why do I feel a strange heaviness? As if my legs are moving forward but my instinct is dragging me back. I have grown up alongside instincts. They tell you whether or not the bull will attack; whether the shadows in the field are thieves or simply rabbit chasers. Over the years, the countryside has taught me never to ignore instincts. But maybe this isn't instinct pulling me back. Maybe I am apprehensive simply because of the stories doing the rounds. There are no ghosts, I almost speak aloud, as if reassuring myself.

I manoeuvre the narrow, curvy path taking care not to let the thorns get my jersey, or my swinging arms. The forest feels much darker than I had thought it would. Stray beams of moonlight seep in through the trees giving the place an eerie feel. Does it always look like this? A mist hangs between the trees and when the moonlight trickles down, it replicates the tiny condensing clouds erupting from my mouth with each breath. As if the trees are breathing.

And what is with this immutable chirr of the crickets? Well, actually it is not the sound I hate as much as the intervening silence. In what feels like a perfectly scheduled move every few minutes, all the crickets instantly stop chirping and the forest is overcome by this surreal, deafening silence. Silence so harsh that it hurts the ears to listen to it. I have to bark a fake cough, or pound the trail harder as I run, to make it go away. The profound stillness of the forest is so intense and overwhelming it feels as if I am being watched through the dark trees.

Contrary to the silence, no matter how softly I try to land, every now and then the dry twigs crack under my feet, suddenly making me jump.

Dry twigs don't make such a big sound in the daytime, do they, I wonder. What is going on? Why does everything feel so unsettling?

The mist in the moonlight makes it feel like the forest is breathing. The silence makes it feel like the forest is listening. The twigs exploding under my shoes make it seem like the forest is talking. Why is this goddamned forest alive! No matter how much I deny it, I am beginning to feel scared. I want to get out of the forest. I make some mental calculations, and realise that I am almost in the middle of the forest. I have no option but to keep moving forward, and hope either for the sun to rise earlier, or for my legs to run faster.

Suddenly, I feel a jab through the sole of my shoe. A massive thorn—the kind I have never seen before—is sticking into the rubber. I pull it off and flick it to the side. 'This is what I don't like about the winters,' I think aloud, 'For most part of the day, it is dark!'

***

I try to act normal and feel normal. But my pulse rate is soaring. I try to remain calm, telling myself it is because of the running. But deep in my heart, I know it is because of the fear I am experiencing. Despite the nip in the early morning air, my brow is beaded with sweat. I realise I am running much faster than intended; almost as if to escape an invisible assailant.

The stories of the villagers keep tossing and turning in my head. Over and over. Like a sleeping giant waking up within me. Before long, I reach a point where I am too scared to even turn around and look. Hysterical and petrified of what I might see, I don't even want to look left or right. Or behind the trees. Or under the bushes. I only want to keep running straight. And out of the forest, as soon as possible.

Hooded figure. The breath in my ears. The skeleton arms. It starts with a series of random words; words from the strange stories of the villagers. Then they slowly form into shapeless thoughts; thoughts that become spectral, incorporeal ideas in my head. And to my horror, very soon, those ideas turn into figures. I keep seeing flashes of the villagers before my eyes. Parsot, the bullock cart driver is there. The grocer. The tea shop owner. Slowly, they all surround me. *Whatever route you take, don't ever take that left after dark!* The villagers keep coming closer. Chanting. Swaying. Chanting. Swaying. Wait, why are they doing this, I ask my horrified eyes. Why are they acting so strange?

'Parsot?' I call out feebly, out of terror. He does not respond. Neither does the grocer. Nor the tea shop owner.

Don't ever take that left after dark... Don't ever take that left after dark... Don't ever... They keep chanting and swaying. And walking towards me. What is happening to them? What are they doing? A million questions fill up my head. It chills my spine, the way they walk towards me. And then a lump forms in my throat when I realise what I am seeing. The villagers are possessed! The chanting pierces through my ears. And the group closes in on me.

'Parsot!' I scream out, getting hold of his arm to shake him awake. But what is this! All I am holding is a skeleton arm. No skin. No flesh. Only bones. I can't see his face, but I can smell the jasmine oil. Then, I begin to hear him breathe into my ear, stiffening the right side of my body with goosebumps.

A shriek escapes my mouth, shaking up the stillness of the forest. And instantly I break out of my blood-curdling fantasy and come back to my senses. I am on my knees. I look around. There is nobody. Neither Parsot, nor the others. Only the dark trees and the silent bushes. Only the crickets playing their mysterious song. And dogs howling occasionally far away in the distance.

I am thoroughly shaken up. When did I go down on my knees? Why don't I remember what happened in the past few minutes. Why did I see the villagers the way I did? And then I feel a massive jolt. Am I possessed?

I get back on my feet. The air around me feels solid. As if the fog I am breathing out is surrounding me. Getting into my lungs. Filling up my head. Choking me. I need to get out of this place, I speak aloud. I realise no words come out of my mouth. Paralysed with fear, I stand up and try to take a few steps.

That is when I see it. At first, it is a shadow—a long, slender shadow of the trees in the filtered moonlight. But there is something queer about it. It is moving! As I strain my eyes in the dark to look closely, I realise it is a figure walking towards me. Appalled, and scared out of my wits,

I stand frozen on the spot, unable to move a limb. The figure has a shawl covering its head and flowing down its torso. *The hooded figure?*

Even as my mouth goes dry and my flesh begins to creep, the figure keeps coming closer and closer. With its steady stride, and brisk movement of the arms, it keeps coming closer until I finally see the face. And then I recognise him! It is dark, but the silhouette of the moustache against the outline of his face is unmistakeable. It is Muchhad, the watchman! A young boy, probably his grandson, is walking with him, holding his hand. I heave a sigh of relief. Warmth returns to my limbs that had gone cold. It feels like I have been given a new lease of life.

Muchhad has the longest moustache in the entire village. A moustache that seems to have an identity of its own; and he proudly twirls it all day long as he sits at the gate of the government primary school. Kids are scared stiff of his look, and that is precisely what makes him good at his job.

'Long time, Muchhad ji,' I greet him more out of delight than anything else. 'How have you been?'

Muchhad doesn't reply. Maybe he doesn't recognise me in the dark, I think to myself. I watch as Muchhad passes me by, without a word, even without looking at me.

Nevertheless, his company feels like a welcome change in the dark, lonely woods. I regain my composure and even find it funny how I got carried away by my own imagination. The barking of the dogs becomes louder, and I feel better, listening to the familiar sounds from the village, which is not far. There are no ghosts. They simply exist in the head. I am going to tell the villagers, I decide, that I ran through the woods in the dark. That there is neither a ghost nor a spirit haunting the woods. I can almost imagine being proclaimed the bravest villager. I can even visualise Parsot's bullock tied to our farm gate. My father will be so proud. I can almost hear stories about myself going around the village. 'That guy who goes running in the mornings? He took that left into the dark woods!'

That is when I hear a soft, low whistle. At first it is very gentle. Then it slowly becomes audible. What a strange bird, I think to myself. At this hour! But I am not scared anymore. I feel proud of myself for not having listened to the naive villagers. But will they all believe that I really did run through the dark, haunted forest? Of course! There was Muchhad! He is my eyewitness.

I turn around to call out a goodbye just to make sure he notices me. My heart jumps to my throat as I see Muchhad standing right there, facing me, looking at me through the darkness. That is when I realise it is he who is making that strange whistling sound.

'Ay Muchhad ji, an early morning stroll? Or are you here on duty?' I laugh.

Muchhad continues making the long, low whistling sound. Is he calling out to me or is this his way of trying to amuse his grandson? Before I can answer myself, he turns around and begins walking away with his boy. I keep looking at them for a while. The reassuring silhouette of a man and his grandson disappearing into the darkness.

I turn around and begin jogging my way out of the forest. I think of old Muchhad and how he has spent all his life at the gate of that primary school. I really hope he remembers that we crossed paths in the forest so that the villagers believe me when I tell them I ran through the woods in the darkness, taking that very left.

As dawn breaks, the forest begins to come alive and seems less daunting with every step. I skip along the narrow route, elated at having proven the ghost stories wrong. The dark trees begin to get back their green. The peculiar mist begins to recede. In a few minutes, the sun will rise and simultaneously I will emerge from the forest, right next to the tea shop. I hope that there will be a lot of customers at the shop so that they all see me walking bravely out of the forest.

The vegetation becomes less dense as I near the edge. Soon, the tall, inhospitable teakwood trees give way to the friendlier chikoo trees. The wild shrubs transform into flowery hedges and the thorny bushes into barbed wire fencing. And before I know it, the narrow unpaved trail ends onto the wide tar-covered road. Like a warrior coming home victorious from a battle, I walk towards the tea shop. I am disappointed to find the place empty, but I decide the tea shop owner is good enough. He will spread the story to the entire village, along with the morning tea.

The owner is indeed shocked and surprised to see me emerge from the forest. 'Where have you been?' he asks me, his eyes wide with horror, as he plucks dry leaves from my hair. I am delighted. My plan is working!

I tell him the entire story while sipping on tea, only leaving out the part where I got scared of my own imagination. That wouldn't go too well with my adventure, I decide.

'You see, I am alive!' I exclaim at the end. 'There are no ghosts and no spirits. They warned me against taking that left. And yet I did it!' I proclaim smugly. 'Muchhad can tell you. He crossed me on the way!'

'Who?'

'Muchhad! The watchman, Muchhad?' I ask, hoping to see a spark of recognition and acknowledgement in the tea shop owner's eyes. Instead, he stares at me blankly, just like Muchhad had, back in the forest. His eyes are stony and vacant. What he says next makes my blood freeze. The tiny cuts and bruises on my skin caused by brushing against the thorns suddenly become prominent as I notice goosebumps form on my forearms.

In a sombre voice laced with a ring of confused angst, the tea shop owner looks into my face and says, 'Muchhad died a year ago!'

***

Back home, at the breakfast table set up on the front lawn, I sit silent and pale, lost in thoughts. I try to strike up a seemingly casual conversation. 'Papaji, do you remember Muchhad?' I ask my father.

'The school watchman, you mean?'

I nod.

'What about him?'

'He hasn't been around since long, has he?' I ask, trying to remain casual. 'I haven't seen him in ages!'

My father continues applying honey on the homemade khakhra sitting on his plate. 'He died a year ago,' he replies nonchalantly. 'Why do you ask?'

'Oh, I didn't know that,' I mutter, trying to hold back the fear palpitating in my words.

'I wouldn't have known either. But there were strange stories...'

I look up, startled, still trying to gulp down that sip of coffee. 'What stories, Papaji?'

When my father replies, a second shiver runs right through my body, chilling my bones.

'They say a young boy from the primary school suddenly died on the same day under mysterious circumstances. The doctor doing the rounds said it was from dengue. But it was all queer!'

***

The thoughts make me shudder. I can swear it was Muchhad, I tell myself for the hundredth time. That moustache was just unmistakeable. And that young boy! Was he the same child who died?

Muchhad's shawl-covered figure plays out before my eyes over and over again, walking towards me holding the boy's hand. Silently. And then, when I turn around, there he is staring right back at me. Could it have been a spirit that I saw? Could he have been the dead Muchhad walking? I suddenly remember the barking of the dogs in the distance. Didn't they say dogs can sense the presence of spirits? A shudder again. Were they both really dead? But I remember noticing the whiffs of mist forming from his mouth! I am left bewildered. I would never be able to tell. The world of spirits is strange. There are no questions and no logic. Only darkness and fear.

I think of Muchhad's long, low whistle. Why was he calling me? Was he trying to say something? What was he trying to tell me? I sit warily in the well-lit living area, too scared to even go upstairs to my room. Like I said earlier, life is much easier when you don't believe in ghosts. I wish I didn't have to believe in them. But now there is no going back. I have no option. I must believe in them, like all the other villagers. And once you start believing in them, you become a part of their strange, eerie, supernatural world. They become a part of you. And you become a part of them. As natural as that.

As much as I wanted to tell you this incident, I do hope that you don't end up believing my story. Because, again, like I always say, life is much easier when you don't believe in ghosts.

As ignorant as I feel saying this, and as strongly as you think of me as a benighted peasant, if there is one piece of advice you ask of me, I would be compelled to tell you this. That, as you go running, whatever route it is that you take, don't ever take that left after dark!

Because if you did, you would believe my story.

***

song of the champions

As a child, every time I had my summer break from school, my mother would take me to the city to visit her parents: my Nana-Nani. They lived in Mumbai, erstwhile Bombay. Even though it was fun being at my grandparents', the city overwhelmed and daunted me, a young farm boy from the countryside. It was a rather formidable place with monstrous buildings instead of tall, slender Asopalav trees; peacefully grazing cows replaced by honking cars; red and green blinking lights instead of the old traffic policeman… My mother said the policeman sat behind the computer screen in his office, and operated the automatic lights. But why! Wasn't it more fun to blow a whistle and wave than sit in an office and turn some silly lights on and off? Also, how would he know if the vehicles were listening to his order or not? And how would he blow the whistle twice and wave back to some old friend passing by the crossroads?

Sitting in the small balcony overlooking the dusty street, sticking my legs out from the cemented grills and swinging them to the tune of my thoughts, I would always wonder what a strange place the city was. They said I couldn't go down to the street and play with the bunch of stray puppies. Instead, they said I could play on the terrace. But how does one play in a place that has a boundary wall around it?

However, despite the absurdity of the place, I did agree to go to the city each summer for two reasons, mainly because of the treats Nana always stocked for me—delightful-looking things that one could only find in the city. And to meet Kaka.

Kaka was this man who looked like a younger version of Nana. They had the same face. The same build. The same hair pattern, and the same smile that seemed to shine more in the eyes than on the lips. He was Nana's younger brother, but I could never decipher how he was related to me. And since my mother called him Kaka, I, too, called him Kaka.

Kaka was a brilliant entertainer. Each morning, he would take me to the giant temple with its tall marble pillars carved to such perfection that I would gaze in awe as I ran my fingers over the imprisoned gods. I liked visiting the temple because that was the only place in the city where one could find a cow. It was always tied to a pillar just outside the temple. Sitting there looking bored, it would simply stare at the passing cars, swishing its tail to ward away flies. Kaka would buy big, brown laddoos from the owner and we would feed them to the cow. It always made me wonder why the owner didn't feed the cow himself. After all, he owned all those laddoos on display, didn't he? Anyway, the city was a strange place. Maybe that is how the city cows liked it.

The best time of the day was the evening. Kaka would be dressed in his crisp white tracksuit, don his crisp white hat, and smile his crisp white smile. We would wait along the parked cars until other kids living in the nearby apartments gathered in the parking compound. Kaka would then organise sprint races for us. We had to run to the old red Fiat parked in the corner, swipe the dust off its body with one finger, and come back to the start. Nobody could cheat, because if you turned around before you got to the red car, you wouldn't have the dust on your finger. Kaka would pitch us against each other, two at a time, gradually clubbing the faster runners together. In the end, the one who could outrun everybody else was declared the champion for the evening.

I still have perfectly vivid memories of those evenings. For they used to be the best evenings I have ever lived. I loved them because I loved to run. Or maybe I loved to run because very often I would be the champion for the evening.

What was most amusing was how Kaka turned the small parking area into a massive stadium. He would stand there leaning against a parked car, and at the call of 'Ready, Steady, Go!' two of us would shoot off towards the opposite end. The other kids cheered us wildly as we touched the red Fiat, swiping off the dust and turning around to run towards the finish line. The excitement was nothing short of running down the home stretch of an Olympic final in front of a thousand wildly cheering spectators. This very feeling drew me to the city year after year.

Residents of the apartments would stand in their balconies to see what the noise was about. A couple of grumpy ones would complain and ask for the games to stop. But nobody dared terminate our fun as long as Kaka was around.

At dusk, we would gather in a circle around Kaka and he would sing us a song. It was more like a poem-song; a Gujarati folk song for kids. It was the same song every evening, and we would all sing along. We called it *Vijeta Geet*: The Song of the Champions.

I don't remember the lyrics completely, but I can hum the tune if you ask me to. And all I can remember from the lyrics is this much:

Let's see you run five miles.

Let's see you pick up a shovel and dig the earth.

Not for the pot of honey, but for the fun.

For when the sun sets, you'll see how happy it makes you.

No, it doesn't rhyme. And not just because it is translated. It didn't rhyme even back then. Not even the original lyrics in Gujarati rhymed. It was the catchy tune that was superlatively captivating. If you heard it once, you were likely to keep humming it all day long ... all through the summer... even when you returned back home after the summer break was over. Today, it is this very song I am desperately trying to recollect, hopelessly racking my brains, as I stand at the foot of his bed, silently looking at the old, frail, sleeping Kaka.

***

As the years passed, I grew up and Kaka grew old. Slowly but surely, we drifted apart. Maybe because the summer vacations became shorter and trips to the city were less frequent. Nana's special treats became available even in the countryside, and the parking area seemed to shrink with each trip, until it finally stopped being the grand Olympic stadium it once was. Maybe it wasn't just I. Because even the other kids no longer found the grandeur that we once sought in those mesmerising evenings. Maybe, being the champion for the evening didn't excite us anymore.

It is astounding what a few years can do to a relationship. For when I went to Nana's place after a long gap, everything about Kaka felt so different. I couldn't jump up and hang onto his back. With the passing years, I had grown taller and his back noticeably weaker. We stopped going down to the Olympic stadium altogether.

So somewhere between my growing up, and his growing old, we grew apart. And just as the distances grew, he grew out of his crisp white tracksuit. And just as I grew into formal shirts and trousers, he grew into the plain white kurta-pyjama that most old people wear. Soon, as much as I hate to admit it, under the building weight of the years, he simply moved away from the Kaka he once was to join that group of distant relatives who you say 'hello' to at weddings, once in five years. And as subtle as it could ever get, without me realising it, even the song of the champions simply faded away into oblivion.

Until the old, old wrinkles on Kaka's sunken face reminded me of it again.

***

He looks so old and shrivelled, it makes me wonder if it is the same tracksuit-wearing, song-singing, Olympics-organising Kaka I am looking at. What a sorcerer Time is. It heals better than anybody else. But when it destroys, it destroys way beyond any scope of repair. I am shocked. How could a few years change so much? His skin looks pale. He bears an uncanny resemblance to a skeleton simply covered with skin. It is a dreadful sight. I want to look away, but my eyes are glued to him.

Plastic tubes go in and out of many different parts of his body. Into his nose, from his wrist, out from the blanket covering his torso. As if he is a lab specimen undergoing a test. His room feels stuffy and hot. The air is filled with the odd smell of hospital wards. Of spirit, medicines, and some more spirit.

It is October. The temperature outside is touching forty degrees Celsius. I can feel sweat trickle down my back at regular intervals. But Kaka is tightly wrapped up in his thick blanket like a newborn baby. Was this what they meant by the cycle of life? That you grow old and become a baby again? What a cruel joke!

I look at his face as he sleeps calmly. His breath is so soft that only the condensation in the plastic tubes and the extremely subtle heaving of his chest under the blanket assure me that he is still breathing. I prop myself against the bed as I wait for him to wake up. My skin touches something warm, and I cringe at the sight of the urine bag hanging at the foot of his bed. I move away slightly.

His attendant sits on a chair next to the head of Kaka's bed. They call him Bahadur. He smiles at me briefly, as I look towards him. 'He should be up any minute now,' he says. I manage to mumble something to the effect of not being in a hurry at all, and remain patiently seated.

He continues talking about how Kaka gets exhausted even when sitting up in bed for half-an-hour. I wish he would speak a bit more softly, or not at all, lest we disturb Kaka. But it seems Kaka will not get disturbed even by an earthquake. Or the cheering from the Olympic stadium in the parking. His eyes remain shut, and he remains motionless as ever.

I am humming the song of the champions in my mind, trying to recollect the lyrics for the tenth time. The tune plays perfectly in my head but the words fail me. I wish I could sing the song for Kaka when he wakes up. I wish I could sing the tune for you through the pages, as you read this story. And have you keep humming it for days. Because that is how indelible the tune is.

Suddenly, I notice that Kaka's eyes are open. I wonder how long ago he woke up. He simply lies in his bed, staring at me, without saying a word. Just that occasional blinking of the eyelids. Bahadur has gone to the kitchen to fetch Kaka's food. I smile at Kaka. He simply stares back, as if I am a stranger. He doesn't seem to recognise me. It shatters me from within, but I keep holding up that light smile against a heavy sense of hopelessness trying to pull it down.

Bahadur returns with a small steel bowl with some white paste in it, and a small steel spoon. He places it on the table next to the bed. 'Do you recognise him?' he asks Kaka, giving him a little shake, talking slowly, as if to a one-year-old. Kaka says something in a whisper that sounds like a blow of breath to me. But Bahadur confirms that Kaka recognises me.

'Do you want to sit up?' Bahadur asks.

Another blow of air. It could have been a yes. And it could have been a no. It wouldn't have sounded any different. And from the pale look on his face, it seems it wouldn't have made any difference either. But Bahadur says it is a yes, so he lifts Kaka's head and helps him into a sitting position, arranging the pillows behind him to prop up his lolling head. With Bahadur's coaxing, Kaka gulps down two spoonfuls of the white paste. He is in excruciating pain and pushes the bowl away, slumping back into the bed, exhausted. He stares at me blankly for a while, and I look back at him. His eyes seem even more deeply set now. As if they are being sucked into the skull. His shaggy, grey stubble is still growing, I notice. His cheekbones look so prominent that his cheeks make a depression on each side like huge craters on a war-torn face.

It does seem Kaka is at war. A war to live on, or perhaps to die. It is a struggle to speak, to eat, to sit up, to smile... Yes, I notice he seems to want to smile at me, but I could be wrong. Again, he wants to say something, but only air escapes his mouth. Bahadur leans closer to him to listen, and Kaka whispers again, but Bahadur still doesn't get it. He hands Kaka a pen and holds up a notepad before his face. With great difficulty, Kaka picks up the pen and scribbles something on the pad. Then he drops the pen and shifts his gaze back to me.

Bahadur lifts the notepad close to his narrowed eyes and wrinkled brow, trying to read. After a futile attempt, he shakes his head, turning the notepad around to see if the letters make any sense. Apparently, they don't. He hands the notepad to me, asking me to give it a try. I peer into the page. It has a few Gujarati letters, but they don't seem to make any words. It seems like a random scribble that is not expected to convey any message whatsoever. I look at Kaka. He still looks back at me with the same grave expression. With the same hopeful eyes. Read it, will you, he begs of me. I look closely again. No. It makes absolutely no sense. I give up. I look back at him helplessly. 'I am sorry, Kaka, I can't understand it,' I tell him. Kaka gives up, too. I see the disappointment in his eyes, and it kills me. It must be an abhorrent damnation to want to share something with the world and have nobody understand you!

I suddenly remember the tune of the song again. I try to distract Kaka out of his sadness. 'Kaka?'

He looks up slightly.

'Do you remember the song of the champions that you made us sing?'

A blank stare.

'Kaka?' I speak louder, and clearer. 'The song of the champions? Do you remember the song of the champions?'

Nothing. Only that grim stare. And the stony eyes. Maybe he can't hear me, I decide. Because if he could, he would surely smile. 'I don't remember the words, Kaka, but I remember the tune very well!' I lean closer, and speak louder.

Still nothing. Does he not remember the song? It was years ago. Maybe he has forgotten it. A wave of disappointment mingled with alarm sweeps through my mind. The song, it seems, is lost forever. For I had asked my mother a dozen times if she remembered the words. She said she had never heard such a song. I had tried googling it. No search results.

I hum the tune in my head again, because that is all that is left of it. It feels amazing simply to sit next to Kaka and play the tune in my head. And suddenly, overcome by emotions, I begin humming it aloud.

Kaka beats the dust off his white track pants, adjusts his hat and draws a line in the dust with the tip of his shoe. The other boy and I stand side-by-side, and Kaka begins to count. 'Ready. Steady. Go!'

And off we go. The other children cheer wildly. They are all cheering for me because I am the faster one. They know I am going to win. And I know I am going to win. And I can simply hang in until we touch the red Fiat, and then accelerate only towards the end to make the race a bit more exciting. The shuffling of the feet raises a sickening cloud of dust as we touch the car and turn around. But dust is good. Dust means you have played. Dust means you have run. Dust means you have picked up a shovel and dug the earth until sunset. Not for the pot of honey. But for the fun. For the happiness it gives you.

Kaka is singing in his tuneless voice. It is hypnotising. After all, it is the song of the champions!

Let's see you run five miles, he sings.

Let's see you pick up a shovel and dig the earth. Kaka looks at me, and smiles. I smile back as I sing along with the other children. The happiness is matchless. You would think it is because I won the race. But I realise the boy who lost to me seems equally euphoric. I don't know why. Perhaps because it is—

Not for the pot of honey, but for the fun.

For when the sun sets, you'll see how happy it makes you.

And then the sun sets.

The colourful lights of the city spring up as it gets dark. The lights from the balconies of the tall buildings make it seem like we are standing at the bottom of a stairway to heaven. The enticing aroma of a dozen different meals being cooked in a dozen different apartments reaches my nostrils and makes my mouth water. I breathe in deeply, and Kaka knows I am hungry.

'Ah, this aroma! This is why I come to the city,' I tell Kaka, jumping up and hanging onto his back. Kaka laughs. He knows why I come to the city. It is because of the sprint races; so I can become the champion for the evening. I come here for the joy of singing at the top of my voice. Most importantly, it is because of Kaka that I come to the city. And he knows it better than anybody else.

Hand-in-hand, we make our way up the six flights of stairs, as the day slowly drags to an end. It has been a spellbinding evening. For a moment it seems as if Time will simply stand still and bear witness to my life. That the sun will halt its journey towards the horizon, and admire the contagiously captivating passion of a dozen children merrily singing a simple folk song with a man in a white tracksuit and a hat.

But Time must move on. And so here I am, sitting with my time-worn, emaciated, weary, old Kaka.

***

I bid Kaka a silent farewell, and leave his room. I take the staircase down to the parking compound. The dusty ground has now been covered with pavement blocks. The old, red Fiat in the corner is gone. A shiny black Mercedes has proudly taken its place. Not even a speck of dust could touch it. Let alone the boisterous fingers of young sprinting lads.

The area looks miserably tiny now. Was this the same Olympic stadium, I wonder? It must be. I had just witnessed Time turn around the life of a fit, tracksuit-wearing man. Surely it could transform an enormous Olympic stadium into a tiny parking lot?

Perhaps it is Kaka's absence that makes all the difference. After all, what is an Olympic stadium without the song of the champions?

Somewhere deep inside my heart, it hurts that Kaka doesn't mean the same to me anymore. That over the years, as I chased bigger joys and struggled to become a champion at life, I forgot the simple joy of being a champion for the evening.

***

Three days later, as we sit outside on the veranda in the evening, my mother receives a call that breaks the news. And our hearts. Kaka passed away peacefully that afternoon. He was at home, surrounded by his family and the people he loved, including the trustworthy Bahadur.

They said his health had improved drastically in the last two days. They even got rid of the feeding tubes. He had asked for the barber to come home and give him a haircut and shave his beard. And he had asked for his favourite *undhiyu* to be cooked that evening. Though he didn't eat much, it was quite a change from feeding tubes to asking for food.

Bahadur is on the line and he says he wants to talk to me. My mother hands me the phone. 'He left you a note,' Bahadur's soft voice comes through the line. 'He spent almost an hour last night trying to put it down.'

'Really? What does it say?'

'The letters are too shaky to make any sense, but it looks like a song...'

My heart skips a beat. 'A song? Are you sure?'

'No,' Bahadur replies. 'I don't know. Because the words don't…'

'…rhyme?' I finish for him.

'Exactly! How do you know? Do you know the song?'

'I don't,' I reply. 'But I need to. Could you keep the note safely for me?'

'Of course.'

I hang up. My eyes are turning moist.

My mother asks me what Bahadur said. I can only wipe my eyes and smile.

I look up. It is evening and the sun is about to set. It is about the same time, isn't it, I think to myself. Time for Kaka's song. I hum the tune aloud. The pink evening sky leans down to listen to it. Just like old times, the sun halts its voyage. And Time pauses its progression.

My mother throws me a puzzled expression. She says she doesn't know the song.

'I don't know it either,' I tell her. 'But I will soon!'

'What song is it?'

I look at her and smile. 'Vijeta Geet—the song of the champions,' I tell her, as yet another tear slides down my cheek. I shut my eyes in pure rapture. And around me, a dozen other children sing along at the top of their voices, tapping their feet to match the beats.

Let's see you run five miles.

Let's see you pick up a shovel and dig the earth.

Not for the pot of honey, but for the fun.

For when the sun sets, you'll see how happy it makes you.

Note after note rises up in the placid October sky through the quiet, dark mantle of the falling dusk.

Kaka leans back on a parked car, straightens his crisp white tracksuit, adjusts his crisp white hat, and smiles his crisp white smile. And then he laughs heartily back at us, as the song comes to a soft end.

Only to start off yet again.

***

a midnight boat ride

You know what they say about the right person showing up in your life at the right time, with the right piece of advice to guide you along the right path?

Well, they are wrong.

I don't believe in it; it has never happened with me. Perhaps it happens in the city, but not here in the countryside. Here, along the narrow Gulmohar-flanked roads, for miles and miles as you run, it is just you and your thoughts. And the carpet of dying yellow-orange flowers for you to tread on. The thoughts keep growing with the distance until they finally consume you. Nobody has come out of the blue with an outstretched hand and a made-to-order piece of advice when I have been down. Each time, it is I who has had to make an effort to get up, find my balance and seek advice.

I had to do this even when I was going through the lowest lows of my life. What I thought could be a beautiful journey was heading towards something that began to challenge my beliefs and faith in everything. It began to gnaw away at the roots of my self-confidence, shattering my dreams.

How did I lose my way? Where was that ray of hope? Where was the silver lining every dark cloud is supposed to have? What I saw was only a long, dark tunnel without a single ray of light at its end.

Five years. That is how long I had side-tracked my career as an engineer to author a book. Not that the book got rejected by a publisher. No; it never even got to that point. It got rejected by my own self. I stopped finding magic in the plot. Day after day, as much as I tried to deny it, I began to realise that the story I had given five years of my life to was not going to turn into a book. But it was a dream I had nurtured for too long. The attachment was too deep; the resultant hurt was devastating.

Initially, I entered a state of denial. I didn't want to believe it is happening. It is just a phase, I told myself. It will surely pass. Some more editing, and the plot was certain to emerge beautifully. The dream unfailingly reignited each morning as I would sit in the dewy garden sipping on coffee, amidst the chirping of the cuckoos and the blooming of the dahlias. I would, yet again, try to weave a spellbinding story, one that touched my soul. I kept scribbling over the old, dull and dust-covered manuscript, trying to bring out the flame I had once seen in it. But I was merely rubbing two stones together for fire, thinking they were flint. No, the cuckoos never came, and the dahlias never bloomed.

I had to let it go. I finally decided that it was over. When I shut the notebook for the last time, it felt like something inside me had died. Something that saw reason in wanting to wake up each morning for the last five years was now gone.

I look at my finger making meaningless patterns in the sand. The sea is all I have to share my troubles with. There is something calming about the sea, isn't there? Perhaps it is that incessant low hum. Or the persistence of the waves. Or the immensity of the waters that somehow makes you feel safe from within. Whatever it is that you have to say, the sea always hears you out. It never interrupts. It never asks you to stop. It peacefully accepts what you have to throw at it. And washes over your feet in return.

It wasn't just the failed writing attempt that weighed me down. For months thereafter, I used running to vent out my emotions. It helped me find equilibrium. For there is nothing more peaceful than the mind of a human body driven to exhaustion. I used running as a medium to get over my sense of loss, to get back my identity, to find another purpose in life, and to wake up each morning with a smile, yet again.

Until one fine day, that, too, was gone.

It started with a simple niggle in my left leg. I didn't pay much heed to it, assuming it would go away. Until one evening when I couldn't take even a step more. I had to hobble back home. I was in denial again. I simply didn't want to accept that I was injured.

I finally consulted a doctor who asked me to rest for four weeks. Those felt like the longest twenty-eight days of my life. On the twenty-ninth day, I laced up, said a small prayer, and walked out. A short, slow walk. All okay. Then a short, brisk walk. All okay. Then a long, brisk walk. Still okay. Then a short, easy jog. Two hundred metres. Three hundred metres. Four hundred. And bam! The pain returned. I was shattered. I can recall the intensity of my emotions in the backdrop of a tranquil sunset, as I sat on a rock clutching my leg.

The doctor asked me to rest for another four weeks. It angered me. It angered me how easily he asked me to extend the layoff. How it didn't matter to him whether I ran or I didn't. It angered me how my not running didn't change anything for the world. How the earth still revolved around the sun. How the universe still moved on. Because for me, my universe seemed to have fallen apart.

The injury kept healing and resurfacing alternately for twelve whole months. Those were testing times. But little did I know that something worse awaited me.

After a year of X-rays, MRIs and multiple consultations, on a hot summer afternoon, I was told that I could perhaps have genetically weak legs. It felt like the sky had come crashing down on my head. I walked out of the clinic, and never saw the doctor's face again.

Fence. A sharp, thorny, barbed wire fence. Day after day, I worked hard to build it around me. It was a strangely barren field I was living on. Nothing seemed to grow there. Not even a stray blade of grass. Only rough, jagged rocks of hatred jutting out of the ground like a monster's jaw. The sunny country trails turned dull and gloomy. Green turned to grey. The crimson sunrise lost its most consistent eyewitness. The golden sunset lost its charm. It merely became the stroke of an hour that signalled the death of yet another day. Old farmers of Umarsadi who once greeted me with a genial wave of their sickles now seemed to whisper among themselves as I passed by their fields. I merely walked, for I couldn't even dream of running.

I disposed of my running shoes, trashed copies of the magazine that had my photograph on its cover page, emptied the showcase of all the trophies I had won, and dug a trench and buried all my memories in it. Only my thoughts and I were permitted to be inside the fencing. I brought home a puppy. A cruel-looking hound. I named him Suspicion. With saliva dripping out of his mouth, he bared his fangs at whoever tried to come into my field. Day after day, he grew …quicker than I had anticipated. And before I knew it, he turned into a full-sized beast. He did a good job keeping people at bay.

I didn't need anybody. I had all the tools I needed in the barn: the tools of jealousy, hatred, resentment. One gloomy morning, I picked up the tools and began digging into the hard ground. It was surprisingly easy. I dug a deep well. And out of the well, whenever I felt thirsty, I drew out buckets-full of self-pity. It quenched my thirst. It felt soothing. The well kept getting deeper with utmost ease, and I kept lapping up the water. I drank to my heart's content. And then I drank some more. And before I knew it, I was high and drunk on the sweet-tasting waters of blame. I blamed people. I blamed Umarsadi. I blamed Fate and I blamed God. I blamed everybody but myself. And it felt good. And as I blamed, I refilled the well every night with my own tears.

One day my mother tried to enter the fence. She crossed over a small bridge that I had never noticed. Maybe she had built it herself. Perhaps it is a special gift mothers are granted. It was a grey, foggy autumn morning and everything was dying. She came around and asked me what was wrong with me. I remember spitting fire at her.

And I remember burning down that last bridge completely. I packed a few clothes and some cash, and left Umarsadi.

I began walking south along the coast of the Arabian Sea. When I got tired, I hitched a ride. When I found none, I hopped onto a bus. At night, I slept on the beach, or in a rented shanty. As day broke, I would set off again. I passed towns and cities with strange names, places I didn't even know existed. I kept close to the sea; somehow I couldn't let go of it. After twelve days, I reached a small fishing hamlet called Malvan. The air smelled of drying fish, and curtains of blue, woven fishing nets hung between tall, gorgeous coconut trees. For some strange reason, arriving there felt like coming home.

And now, here I was, facing the sea, crying into the sunset, and making pointless patterns in the wheatish-brown sands of Malvan beach.

***

Genetically weak legs.

The words keep getting louder and louder in my ears. I tried to shut out the sound by shutting my eyes and focusing on the waves. But the sound of those words rose above the rumble of the sea, like an evil spell somebody had cast on me.

I began to loathe what running had done to me. It had made me dream and then it had dropped a bomb of cruel reality on my head. I had become a slave to running. I depended on it for my happiness. I was trapped in my shoes. I couldn't run, but somehow it was all I wanted to do. I couldn't stop, but I had to. I had come too far to turn back now.

It all feels gloomy. The low roar of the sea. The whistle of the wind. It feels like I have nowhere to go. Nobody to turn to. I suddenly miss my mother. I wish I had a phone. I wish I could call her and tell her that I missed her. That I loved her. That I was sorry.

It kills me to think I had snapped back at her angrily like I had. Inebriated as I am from the emotional turmoil, a wave of guilt washes over me, and tears come spewing out of my eyes. I hardly have anything to look forward to in life, and I had just turned away my biggest support. My mother.

In the spur of the moment, with tears blurring my vision, I begin to run. I don't know what I am thinking. But stripped down to my true inner self, raw and helpless as ever, equal parts fragile and broken, this is all I can muster. I run harder than I ever could have. Than I ever should have. Like a drug addict fighting for one last ounce of his drug. Like a survivor battling to breathe. Like a lost child crying for his mother, I cry for mine. I only need to talk to my mother.

I forget all about the injury until half a kilometre later, when it begins to throb. I still don't stop. I would rather run while I can, because soon I won't be able to. I push until I stop feeling sensation in my arms. It comes sooner than I expect. A vicious reminder that I haven't run in months. It is a beautiful feeling, though. Oh, how I missed it. It takes away my limbs, my body, my senses. And I still don't stop. I continue dwelling in that sadistic pleasure. Because it beats down months of piled up frustration that has been ruling over me. I keep running, like I have time only until the sun sets to see as much of the world as I possibly can. As if I have only a few dying seconds to romance this beautiful feeling until it vanishes for good, taking away with it the beautiful life, laughter and all my dreams.

Then, spent and broken, I stop, bending over to catch my breath. Bending over and feeling my injury, as the barbed wire fence begins taking shape around me once again.

That is when he arrives on the scene, smiling ear to ear, breathing hard. 'That was a great run, wasn't it?' he doubles over next to me, visibly delighted with his running.

I don't want to talk to anybody right now. I am a mess. My cheeks are still streaked with tears. I merely smile and turn away from him, hoping the tears will pass for sweat.

But then he says something that makes me turn towards him.

'You run beautifully,' he tells me, his nostrils flaring as he pants.

I don't know what exactly he means. Is he talking about my speed? My form? My strides? I don't know. But the kindness crumbles me. I look up to see if he really means it. That is when I see him for the first time. He must be in his thirties. Not very tall, five feet six, dark complexioned; his long, grizzly hair is tied back in a bun. Rough stubble runs over his prominent chin. His eyes look calm, and his lips are smiling. Standing there against the last rays of the setting sun, he looks every inch a local.

There is something about his looks that tempts me to talk to him. It could be the sand sticking to his face, or the stray hair blowing in the wind, or the glow in his eyes. Or it could well be the effect of the short run. His vibes make me feel better. Perhaps because he was the first person talking to me in almost two weeks, without wanting to sell me fish, temporary tattoo stickers, a taxi ride or a room to stay in.

'I haven't run in a while,' I sigh, just short of breaking down before a complete stranger.

'Doesn't look like it. I had a hard time keeping up!' he replies.

After a brief pause, he offers me a handshake. 'Mantez,' he says. 'Nice meeting you.'

***

For the hundredth time, I wonder what I am doing in a stranger's boat in the middle of the night.

However, in an inexplicable manner, sitting in the makeshift wooden craft amidst the stillness of the moonlit sea, with this man who calls himself Mantez, seems like the right thing to do.

I look at his silent silhouette. I can't see his eyes, and I wonder if he has fallen asleep. Just then, as if to clear my doubt, he gives the oars a gentle row. It doesn't do much to our boat. It only stirs reluctantly, and then settles comfortably over the still waters yet again.

For a long time, there is silence. Even the sea is unusually quiet. Only the gentle waves touching the boat and the occasional splash of water around us every time a fish breaks the surface compel Mantez to ask me: 'Do you hear the fish playing with the waves?'

Yes, I nod.

Apart from that, there is silence. I am not complaining, though. It is a beautiful feeling listening to the moonlight-soaked tranquillity floating on the sea. And Mantez has given me a lot to think about.

'I am a painter,' he had told me earlier that evening. 'I hand-paint designer tiles. I opened my own studio just yesterday, after trying for years.'

That is what endeared him to me. I am fascinated by those who the world calls baseless dreamers, hopeless romantics and passionate lunatics. It felt as if he were the only person I needed to be with in that moment. No, I did not want anything from him; not even advice. He would never understand what I was going through. And I wasn't going to tell him. Yet his mere presence felt comforting. Maybe because all this while I had yearned for someone between a friend and a perfect stranger. And Mantez was just that.

'It is so difficult to become successful, isn't it?' I had asked.

He remained silent for a while. 'That depends on what you call success,' he finally uttered. 'Is success for you the same as what it is for the world?'

I hadn't known what to reply. Wasn't success the same for everyone? If they saw you doing well, they lauded you and called you successful. Before I could reply a yes, he started talking.

'Because if you say "yes", I am sorry, brother, I won't agree. Why do you need the world to call you successful? Why do you need the validation of people?' He paused, half expecting an answer, as he sipped out of his beer can. Then he continued, 'I urge you to go out there and do what you like. Define your own success. For that is where true happiness lies. Let the world point at you and laugh. You play your part. And if the world still doesn't acknowledge your success, come back to me. I shall welcome you with open arms, and trust me, brother, there will be a hundred other people with me. That I can promise you.' Then in two gulps, he finished the beer and tossed the can to the side.

His words were like balm to my wounds. I wanted to tell him my story but I held back my emotions. Just as I had all these months.

The sea was rough. In the dying daylight, the waves crashed against the shore angrily. The wind blew as if in a hurry to get somewhere. And the sea roared louder than ever.

'I feel so small before the sea,' I had told him. 'So insignificant.'

'We are indeed minuscule,' he replied with a broad smile. And then he said something beautiful.

'Sometimes,' he said, 'we need the roar of the blue sea, the vastness of the limitless sky, and the crashing waves at the shore to remind us we are just that speck of sand on the beach...' Silence. 'And sometimes, we need them all to remind us that perhaps we *are* the roar of the blue sea, the force of the crashing waves, and as limitless as the sky!'

And as if the wind had heard him, as if by magic, the tide began to turn. The crashing waves began to subside, as darkness began to envelop us.

'Would you like a boat ride?' he asked me.

Yes, I nodded and smiled.

***

I thought it would be a thirty minute ride; an hour at the most. But it is late and I only want it to go on forever. There is a sense of belonging I feel sitting cross-legged over the wooden framework of the wobbly boat, with Mantez in front of me. It seems strange to think that I had only met him that evening. It feels like I have known him for a lifetime. I bend over and touch the cool water of the sea. It beats me how the sea could feel so calm. It is all so still. So quiet. So dark and lonely. It almost makes me feel scared.

'Mantez?' I call through the dark.

'Yes?'

'Do you ever feel scared?'

'Scared?'

'Yes. Scared of being all by yourself in the sea?'

Mantez chuckles. 'I grew up here, brother. How could I ever be scared of the sea?'

'No, I don't mean it that way. Do you ever get scared of…' I pause, thinking. '… of life? As if you are all alone in the world. All by yourself...' I explain.

Mantez remains silent for a while. I hear his breath from across the boat in the darkness. He lets go of the oars for a moment, stretches his arms above his head, and replaces them on the sides of the boat. Then, with the firmness of the rocks at the shore, he says, 'You are never alone, my friend!'

It is as if he is stating a universal fact. A perfectly irrefutable gospel. Such is the solemnity of his tone.

'I will tell you a story from when I was young, if you want to hear it.'

'Go on.'

'My father was an artist. He never wanted me to follow a conventional path. He wanted me to live my dreams. 'Don't die with the wild still in you, son!' he would always tell me.'

Mantez continues. 'But the world is big and scary, isn't it? It is difficult to follow the trail when everyone else is taking the highway. The trail is lonely and intimidating.'

I nod in the dark. I know that feeling too well. For a moment it makes me wonder if Mantez knows what I am going through.

'My father always knew how scared I felt in life. He knew I wouldn't have the courage to stand up for my dreams when the time came. So one day he asked me to follow him to the sea on a dark night. I must have been eighteen at that time. Or nineteen. I still remember that night very vividly. We walked along the shore in silence. There was no moon in the sky, and I could barely see a thing ahead. And then my father tapped me on the shoulder and asked, 'Are you scared?'

'No,' I replied.

'Why?' he asked me.

I thought for a moment. 'Because I am not alone!'

'Well, you should know one thing, son.'

'What, Papa?'

'You will *never* be alone!'

'I didn't understand what he meant. But he asked me to keep walking, so I did. We walked until we reached the end of the beach, where the marshy backwaters began. Then out of the bushes, he began to pull out a boat. Oh, it was this very boat we are sitting on tonight.'

'What are you doing, Papa,' I asked.

'He didn't reply. He kept pulling the boat into the swamps. When the boat began to float, he asked me to hop on to it. I was bewildered, but I did as I was told.'

'I am going to blindfold you and leave you floating here,' he told me, to my utter trepidation. 'If you think you are man enough to follow your dreams, you will leave the blindfold on all night, until the first rays of the sun glow through it.'

'I looked at my father to see if he was joking. The marshes are where the most terrifying of sea creatures live—the crocodiles, the scorpions and the water snakes. Surely he couldn't be serious! But his expression was grave and humourless. I was too scared to disobey him. So I let him blindfold me.'

'What happened then?' I ask.

'I sat there all night in the boat, scared out of my wits. Every time I heard the water swish, or I felt the boat move, I thought it was an alligator coming to get me. I imagined poisonous snakes crawling into the boat. I could hear nocturnal animals crying around me all night. It was the scariest night of my life. I felt so lonely and frightened.'

'Did you manage to stay the night?

'I did!' Mantez cries, jubilant. 'But guess what happened when the daylight finally showed up!'

'What?'

'I opened the blindfold, and to my surprise, I saw my father sitting right next to me in the boat! He had been sitting there all night, protecting me from harm!'

A gasp escapes my mouth. And then a smile. What a beautiful experience; what an enchanting story!

'That day my father taught me an important lesson. 'Keep the faith strong,' he told me. 'Even when you can see nothing, believe that you are not alone. Keep your belief strong, even when your vision fails you!' It sounds like just another piece of advice, doesn't it? But believe me, if you had lived through that night, it would have changed everything about your beliefs. Because since that day, I have never felt lonely, or scared. Because I know I am never alone!'

Mantez lets the silence take over again; lets the idea sink into the realm of my understanding.

Then he asks, 'Do you hear the fish playing with the waves?'

This time I don't reply. A massive wave of change is washing over me. And bathing in its discerning enlightenment, I am experiencing the most heavenly feeling I have felt in months.

***

It is way past midnight. It seems like we just spent an hour on the boat, but now the moon has moved a lot more towards the west, and the stars have visibly shifted by a dozen degrees. It makes me wonder what time the clock would show. One? Two? And yet, nothing about the night has changed. The same gentle waves. The same sound of the fish.

'It is late,' Mantez finally announces. He begins to row us towards the shore, and the sleeping boat follows his commands, dragging itself over the soft waves. Soon the lights at the shore finally come into sight. A gleaming set of diamonds along the coast. A glimmering reminder that the world is still alive.

But it isn't the same world that we had left behind when we set off in the boat. It feels like a completely different one. It is beyond my understanding how a few hours with a complete stranger can transform what I thought about the world. And myself. It is fascinating how a simple boat ride could change my perception of life.

'This was nothing short of a beautiful dream,' I tell Mantez as we step onto the soft, wet sand of Malvan.

'Well, then,' Mantez replies with a smile, 'before you wake up, let me repeat that tiny piece of advice.'

I look towards him longingly. 'You were born to run free, my friend,' Mantez says. It really gets my attention. Run free? Did he mean it in the literal sense? How did he know? I am surprised, but I continue to listen.

'You were born to run free. You were born to climb mountains and catch the magical sunrises. To play with the wind. To fall asleep under the canopies of rain trees. You were meant to work hard. To fall. To get back up. To laugh through it. To run again. It is the experience that counts. Everything you collect in life…' he stops, bends down, and picks up a seashell from right under his foot '…is always an exquisite souvenir from this sandy journey of life!'

Then almost in a whisper, he speaks, as if thinking of the night with his father all over again. 'Go on. Live as hard as you can. And don't die with the wild still in you!'

I am left rooted to the spot, and swept off my feet, both at the same time. I am out of words. Out of feelings to express myself. The soft sand seems to be sinking, and again I wonder if I would suddenly jerk open my eyes and find myself on my bed, woken up from a dream.

The soft breeze continues to kiss my sand-covered face. The calm sea bids a silent goodbye. Mantez turns around with a smile and walks away into the Malvan darkness. I watch him silently as the night engulfs him in the distance. As if he never existed. As if I was indeed in a dream.

You know what they say about the right person showing up in your life at the right time, with the right piece of advice to guide you along the right path?

Well, they are right!

***

a glass of milk

A delay of even ten minutes for my morning run means I have to take a different route to avoid him. He sits in his stinking corner under the biggest banyan tree that the whole of Umarsadi has to offer; not that Umarsadi is geographically a massive area. Quite on the contrary. But the tree stands out as a spectacular landmark that one just can't miss.

He sits there with his crooked nose, deeply set eyes, thick lips, his long hair in dreadlocks, much like the overhanging roots of the banyan tree, and his shaggy unshaven beard. Every time one passes him, he bellows at the top of his voice, occasionally giving a chase, even hurling stones and abuse. More than the odour of his unwashed body, it is the fear that keeps me from taking that route. A mad beggar running after you at six in the morning isn't the ideal beginning to the day, is it?

He suddenly appeared in the village two months ago. Nobody knows where he came from. He wanders around the village looking for scraps of food in the garbage when hungry, and spends the rest of the time under the banyan tree. He sits there all day, staring into space and talking to himself. At times he makes patterns in the air, as if trying to catch his words. As it gets dark, he gathers his belongings—a soiled blanket, a plastic bowl, and a cane—and hobbles down to the sweet shop in the village to spend the night outside its closed shutters. Sharp at six in the morning, he returns to the banyan tree.

It is a spectacular and majestic tree, that banyan. They say it is five hundred years old. I don't know if it is true, but it does have the character of an old, wise man. The long roots hanging from the branches touch the ground and create the impression of the white beard of a saint lost deep in mediation, even as birds nest in his hair. The trunk is so thick, a cow could easily hide behind it, and the perplexed farmer would walk right by, looking for her.

As I run by, I often find myself throwing a wistful glance at the tree. Before the mad beggar inhabited the place, it was a ritual for me to sit under the tree to catch my breath and sip on coconut water after I finished running. I would often lie on my back admiring the vastness of its canopy. On some days, after a particularly tiring run, I would doze off until the dry leaves crunched under me when I moved, waking me up. All the while the summer breeze would caress my face and ruffle my hair. Sometimes a koel would coo loudly and I would tease it with an identical coo, until it got annoyed and flew away to another tree. Oh, those delightful days!

But now, the mad beggar occupies the space. Children are asked to keep away from the banyan tree when he is around. And what is a banyan tree without children taking turns to swing on its roots? The lonely tree stands alone day after day, casting a forlorn look, like an old grandpa waiting for his grandchildren to return from school. But the children never return. They are scared of the mad beggar. Of his dreadlocks and his bearded face. Of the way he yells at anybody passing by. Last month, the constable from the local police station had driven him out of the village, but the stubborn beggar returned to the tree two days later. The constable said he didn't get paid enough to drive anybody out of the village twice. It sounded funny to me, but the villagers thought of it as a valid explanation. And so, the mad beggar stays put under the banyan tree.

***

It is a crisp, cool November morning. The kind where fearless dew drops sit majestically on tender blades of grass, turning the yellow shafts from the morning sun to a dazzling gold. It will remain so at least until the next one hour, long enough for me to finish my run. But I am ten minutes late, and I will have to run past the mad beggar.

I am about to make a detour when, from a distance, I notice something queer. It is a bicycle parked under the banyan tree. Now this is odd, I think to myself. Who will stop by the tree at this hour?

Cautiously, I creep closer to take a look. And then I notice the colourful tyres of the bicycle. This has to be Jeevan! He is the only person in the village with colourful bicycle tyres. He painted them himself, and when the bicycle moves, the colours spin to form a rainbow until they finally mix up and turn black as the wheels gather speed.

It is Jeevan indeed, the new shepherd in the village. He hails from Saurashtra, a quiet province in the western part of India. The previous monsoon had been very poor in their region, forcing almost everyone to migrate. Jeevan, too, moved out with his family of thirty-six cows and three people. After forty days of walking, they happened to reach Umarsadi. Perhaps the dense coconut plantations by the sea caught his fancy. Or perhaps it was the massive banyan tree that made him decide. But he stayed back. A generous farmer lent Jeevan a small portion of his land to keep his cows and build a hut for his family. And with his smiling eyes and the sweetness of his north-Gujarati dialect that is rather uncommon, he managed to win over the villagers. He is a happy man, that shepherd. Nothing about the way he dresses up, or the way he talks, or the way he smiles ever betrays his ordeals in life. And if you casually happen to ask him how he is doing, he would smile the widest smile that anybody with tobacco-stained teeth would dare to smile and say, 'It is all great, Bapa. First class. Top notch. With your blessings and the grace of the Almighty, it is all going great.' That is just how he is.

But does he not know that the mad beggar has to be left alone? I rush to the spot just in time to see the mad beggar getting up, waving his arms angrily and chasing Jeevan away with a stone in his hand.

'Jeevan!' I cry out from where I am standing. 'Watch out, Jeevan!'

He hurriedly mounts his bicycle, and without bothering to sit on the saddle, pedals furiously until he reaches a safe distance. The alarmed milk cans hanging by the sides of his rear tyre rattle in protest as he grinds to a halt next to me. We watch the mad beggar walk back to his place under the tree muttering to himself, shaking his head from side to side.

'What were you doing, Jeevan? He is not a good guy. Just leave him alone.'

'I thought the poor guy must be hungry. I got him some milk, Bapa,' Jeevan replies.

'Are you crazy, Jeevan? He is a mad beggar. Nobody talks to him.'

Jeevan shrugs nonchalantly. 'Maybe *that* is why he is a mad beggar!'

I shake my head out of exasperation and begin walking away. 'You can't go about helping people at the cost of getting struck on the head with a stone, Jeevan. The world will eat you up.'

***

The following day, I see Jeevan with the mad beggar again. I don't bother to stop today. I have warned him. He can do what he pleases.

Even before I make my usual detour, I hear a shriek. I turn around to see Jeevan running to his bicycle, his shirt dripping with milk, and the mad beggar shouting angrily at him. Serves him right, I snort to myself. But Jeevan learns nothing from his experiences with the mad beggar. He remains the same naive, witless peasant. A little too sweet. A little too kind. A little too hopeful for his own good.

The next morning I see him there again.

I don't know how many glasses of milk Jeevan has wasted, or how many shirts he has got drenched in milk, but I start hearing stories from the villagers about how Jeevan talks to the mad beggar every single morning.

'He will go crazy himself if he spends too much time with that madman!' they laugh.

But Jeevan does not mind it one bit. He simply laughs along and keeps going to the mad beggar to waste a glass of milk each morning. As for me, I simply stop taking that route. Winter has set in and because the dawn is delayed, I step out of the house much later. In any case, I want to see neither the crazy beggar nor the crazier Jeevan trying to befriend him.

'You are simply being irrational, Jeevan,' I tell him one day when we cross paths. 'That man is never going to change. He is mentally unstable.'

Jeevan smiles at me but doesn't remain silent. With that same conviction with which he goes to the mad beggar every morning, he tells me something I have never before considered.

'Look,' he places his palm gently on my shoulder. He is standing so close to me, I can smell the cows off his white, sweat-stained shirt. 'I can offer a small piece of advice that I learnt from experience back home, when we were struggling through the drought.'

I press my lips together and hold myself back from impatiently brushing away his hand. 'What is it?'

'When you sow rice and it doesn't grow, you blame the soil and the lack of water. Alright? But God be damned if you ever blame the rice grains, Bapa...'

Saying that he tightens the knot on his turban and walks away, leaving me bewildered.

***

Days turn into weeks, and weeks into months a lot faster than they are supposed to. Winter turns into a short spring before relapsing into a hot, never-ending summer. The mangoes turn from shy little green beads to haughty yellow, pulpy masses hanging from trees. After I return home from my travels, I am eager to set out for an early morning run. That is when I suddenly remember the mad beggar. I look at the watch, and heave a sigh of relief. He wouldn't have arrived at the tree yet. I can safely take my usual running route.

I pass by the banyan tree. Its leaves rustle in the gentle early morning breeze. I am lost in thought as I soak in my scenic surroundings. Rising smoke from the burning wood in most huts along the road, and the scampering chicken around them, subtly announce the arrival of the morning.

A few kilometres down the road, as I turn the corner of an abandoned barn, I fail to notice a sleeping dog curled up by the side of the road. Alarmed, he yelps out in surprise. It is then that I notice something that makes my blood freeze. It isn't just one dog. Huddled together among dry leaves are four huge mongrels!

I am so close I have no time to react. In an instant, they surround me, growling menacingly. I shout as loud as my hysterical voice permits. But what can merely qualify as a squeal escapes my throat. In support, other dogs from the village join them and a deafening cacophony of growls and barks emerges.

I bend down and pick up a stone. What happens in the next few seconds seems like a blur. One of the dogs pounces at me and manages to rip off my shorts. I scream while the pack growls more menacingly. In a futile attempt, I desperately stamp my feet to ward them off. A cloud of dust rises through the darkness. And then the bicycle.

A passer-by, shouting loudly, rides his bicycle straight into the pack of dogs. All at once, the dogs disperse. For the next few minutes, all that is audible is my heart beating against my eardrums. I am in a stupefied daze. When I return to my senses, I see the man on the bicycle smile at me.

The dogs are gone. 'Be safe!' he calls out to me in Gujarati, and turns to leave.

In the dim morning light, before I can recognise him, he pedals away without another word. It is then that the multi-coloured tyres of the bicycle suddenly catch my eye.

'Jeevan! Jeevan!' I shout after him as he disappears into the distance.

❋❋❋

Finishing the run, I take the dirt road to Jeevan's place. The sun is rising up in the sky, the proud dewdrops have perished and activity in the village has long begun. The same stray dogs are basking in the sun on a heap of sand.

I wonder if Jeevan will be home.

I jump over the bales of hay marking the boundary of his piece of borrowed land. The place is littered with cow dung, and smells of a mixture of dry fodder, cows, and the smoke from burning wood. I don't really know why, but it puts a smile to my face. I breathe in deeply. This is the smell of childhood. I love being here for the smell. Or perhaps for Jeevan's hospitality.

Jeevan is squatting near the open porch, milking one of his cows. 'Aavo, padharo Bapa!' he welcomes me cheerfully, urging me to take a seat next to him.

I am reminded of how he had welcomed me the last time I was here, and a smile escapes my lips. 'I am a small man,' he had said in his dialect that was hard to perceive, 'but if you happen to come home I will treat you with so much honour that if you were a God, you would forget going back to your heaven!' He was right. He wouldn't let me leave before I had had two tummy-fulls' worth of lunch. Or perhaps three. Thick, freshly made jowar chapattis served right off the wood-fired stove with a bowl of molten ghee. Chapattis that smelt so delicious, you would rather burn your tongue than wait for them to cool on the plate. I poured ghee over the chapatti. 'No, no, this isn't how you eat it,' Jeevan stopped me. 'You don't put ghee on the chapatti, you dip the chapatti in ghee, Bapa!' It was the best meal ever.

I squat on the mud floor next to Jeevan. Curiously, I peer into his face.

'Is anything wrong, Bapa?'

'Was someone using your cycle early this morning?'

'It must have been Amar.'

'Amar?'

'Amar! Don't you know him? The madman who used to sit under the banyan tree…'

'What! You are joking, right?'

'No, why will I do that, Bapa? Didn't you hear about him?'

I shake my head. 'I had gone to Mumbai, and returned just yesterday. What happened to him?'

Jeevan smiles, showing me his tobacco-stained teeth. He calls out to Amar. 'See for yourself!' he tells me.

I can barely believe what I see. From the hut emerges the very same person who had saved me this morning! It is the mad beggar minus his dreadlocks and his beehive-beard! He is wearing a stained white shirt, just like Jeevan. When he comes closer, I recognise that face—the crooked nose, the thick lips, and the deeply set eyes. Yes, it is him, indeed! The mad beggar! Jeevan laughs at my bewilderment, and Amar shyly turns around and disappears into the hut.

'How... What... How did this happen?' I stumble for the right words.

'It is a long story, Bapa,' Jeevan lets out a sigh of satisfaction. 'I tried talking to him, remember?'

I nod.

'Well, turns out, it worked. He wasn't mentally retarded. He had been abused and traumatised for too long. Poor guy, he was disowned by his family and that really drove him crazy. All he needed was a glass of milk, Bapa.'

I don't get it. 'A glass of milk?'

'In Saurashtra, we say that a glass of warm milk each day can cure any illness. So I tried it. And it worked!' Jeevan chuckles as he adjusts his turban, and begins milking his cow again.

I open my mouth to say something, but there is really nothing appropriate I can say. I don't know if it was the warm milk or simply Jeevan's warmth and kindness, but it changed someone's life. It transformed a mad beggar into Amar.

'He was an angry person,' Jeevan explains. 'It wasn't easy. He gave me a tough time in the beginning. But slowly I befriended him and gained his trust. He seemed to be getting better with each passing day, so I stuck to my routine of getting him a glass of milk every morning.'

'I can't believe it worked, Jeevan. I thought you would give up.'

'No, no, Bapa, come to think of this. You throw stones at someone, you get stones back. But have you ever tried offering them milk?'

I remain silent. Even though it is a general question, I feel the prick of the arrow aimed at me. I find it difficult to look into his eyes that are now smiling.

'And Amar stays with you now, does he?' I ask.

'Yes, he delivers the milk for me. Everyone in the village knows him. They can't believe he is the same mad beggar. Amar is like a younger brother to me now, Bapa.'

I shake my head in disbelief. You could call it a miracle, or a mere coincidence. Proclaim it to be a medical wonder, or pass it off as the work of destiny. But for the rest of his life, Jeevan will only believe in that glass of milk.

Amar, the mad beggar, delivering milk for Jeevan. And saving strangers from a pack of stray dogs. Smiling dreamily to myself, I get up to leave.

'Come to think of it,' Jeevan says softly. 'When my family had nowhere to go, someone was kind enough to let me stay here... And so, I am simply passing on the good deed, Bapa.' He pauses for a second, and I notice his eyes turning moist. Using the pretext of wiping his hands, he wipes his tears, and continues, 'Remember, my friend, in this world, there will always be stones for stones, and kindness for kindness!'

Then, in his sweetly persuasive voice, he asks, 'Won't you have ghee-chapatti before you leave, Bapa?'

***

I reach the old banyan tree. It welcomes me with open arms. It fills my heart with some kind of warmth I never knew I would feel again. I take a seat under its giant canopy. The sun shines down over me through the gaps in the branches above. Three children take turns to swing on the overhanging roots. I have been waiting for this sight since ages. It is like a beautiful snippet from some old reminiscences. Like living through an age-old black-and-white photograph. I breathe a sigh of contentment. I am home.

I shut my eyes and stretch my back on the ground. The dry leaves crunch under my weight. It feels like music to my ears. The air is resplendent with the chirping of sparrows and the delighted chatter of the children as they swing. The old, old banyan tree seems to smile down upon us. The grandchildren are back. And the old grandpa is happy.

As I close my eyes, the mad beggar's face appears before me. It transforms into Amar's face and seems to say to me:

All you need is a bit of love.

And as I slowly drift away into a gentle slumber under the five-hundred-year-old banyan tree, I can't help but acknowledge how funny it is that I needed a cow-herder all the way from drought-stricken Saurashtra to come and explain this simple concept to me.

That when you sow rice, and it doesn't sprout, you don't blame the grains.

You simply water it with a few drops of kindness.

After all, what the world needs is a glass of milk, Bapa.

***

'draw a chair, Munnu!'

I stare dreamily at the eighty-year-old creased piece of paper in my hands. It brings a smile to my face. It is a certificate; a bravery award. A recognition from the village panchayat. It is torn from the sides, and is yellowing with age, but the letters stand clearly legible.

It bears my name.

'I must show this to Munnu,' I speak aloud, holding on to the recent discovery from the depths of the old drawers that I had begun to clean up. 'He will love it!'

I blow away at the dust that has settled on it over eight decades and smoothen out the wrinkles from the piece of paper, holding it close to my heart. I wish I also knew where the medal was, I think to myself. But this old head is losing its memory. I will probably never find it. Maybe it was dumped in that chest in the loft? Or in the cupboard?

I hobble across the room, towards the brown metal cupboard in the corner. It looks old. It *is* old. Flakes of paint are peeling from its surface, and the edges have begun to rust, but the mirror on its door is just as sparkling as it was eighty years ago.

Eighty years? Eight whole decades? Was it really that long ago? I look at my reflection in the mirror. A ninety-year-old face marred by wrinkles looks back at me. It is only the toothless smile that makes me look better.

I think of how I will smile after showing the certificate to Munnu. Tell me more about it, Dadaji, he will say, his eyes brimming with pride and fascination.

Draw up a chair and sit close to me, Munnu, I will tell him. Sipping on the mint sherbet, sitting out in the veranda, I will start my story.

Aided by my dependable walking stick, I shamble out of my room, looking for Munnu. It is funny, isn't it, how humans start off by crawling on all fours as infants, then switch to two, and then to three when they are old, I think to myself, as I support my old body with the stick. I must put this across to Munnu as a riddle; I bet he will not be able to guess the answer!

'Munnu, what is that thing that walks on four legs when young, then on two, and on three when it is old?'

'Humans, Dadaji; you have asked me this a hundred times!'

Have I already, I ask myself. Ah, this old brain is losing its memory. I must come up with newer riddles, and write down the ones I have already asked Munnu. Never mind, I have to show Munnu the certificate. And I have a story to tell him!

'Look what I found, Munnu!'

Munnu gives the certificate a cursory glance and then goes back to looking at his phone. Maybe the old look of the certificate doesn't appeal to him. I will read it out to him. And if he asks, I will tell him the whole story.

Now, where did I put my glasses again? Maybe I left them in my room. Never mind, I will simply tell him the story.

'Draw a chair, Munnu, and sit down next to me, will you? Let me tell you a story!'

'Dadaji, you will have to make it a little quick. I am getting late for my run!' Munnu says. Is it my imagination, or does he really sound a little impatient every time?

'Okay, I will make it quick, Munnu. We don't need the mint sherbet right now if you are in a hurry. We could just sit outside in the veranda. It is a beautiful day. No? You say you are getting late? Okay, we will sit right here, and I will tell you the story. A story about my brother and me.'

***

'It is a wonderful day to swim, isn't it?' Bhalu announces, stretching himself in the summer sun. Bhalu was my brother. No, you haven't seen him. But we were very much alike. You would have liked him, I am sure.

The sun is shining, the sky is blue, and I have to agree with him. The day does look inviting. We change into shorts and make our way to the sea.

I am talking about a time when Umarsadi was only a dense jungle beyond that bridge over the river. There were no houses beyond the Pardi railway station—no people, no roads, no vehicles—only an occasional horse cart clinking away along the narrow dusty trail. Nobody dared to travel alone, and even in a group, you were advised to get back home before five in the evening. Else, you would be looted by bandits. Horse cart drivers would charge twice the fare to cross the forest and take you to the sea. At that time, the fare was one anna.

Do you know how much one anna is, Munnu? Sixteen annas make one rupee. So you can do the math. That was how cheap things were back then. Do you know how much our school fees was, Munnu? It was free for girls and for boys it was...

Sorry? You say I have told you this a dozen times already? This old head, I tell you ... it is losing its memory.

Anyway, I will continue with the story.

Where was I? Yes, so Bhalu and I make our way towards the sea. It is just us running through the jungle, like two petrified boys who had just seen a ghost.

Are you listening, Munnu? What do you keep looking at on the screen of that phone? You are looking at me, you say? Is it just my eyes? I am sorry, I left my glasses in the room. I wouldn't know even if you simply ran away!

I am not boring you, am I, Munnu? I keep getting carried away.

So, yes, both of us are scared of running through the dense forest, but neither of us wants to admit it. And so, with a silent prayer on our lips, we run as fast as our legs can possibly take us. Not because we want to beat each other, but because we are scared of the bandits!

The summer heat ensures we are perspiring even before we are halfway there. We cross over the bridge, stopping for a moment to look at our dancing reflections in the waters below. Then we enter the forest. It is a lot cooler inside and we sprint along the winding trail. We slow down only when we reach the fishermen's huts, relieved to have made it through the treacherous woods. Hands on our knees, we take a moment to catch our breath.

'If not the bandits, running this hard will kill you both one day,' the old, squatting fishermen tell us as they smoke their bidis. We merely laugh and walk away. We would do this every day, merely for the thrill. And for the dip in the sea.

We walk to the beach, dress down to our briefs and place rocks over our clothes to keep the wind from taking them away. We then draw a starting line in the sand, and at the count of three, race like mad dogs into the water. And as we dive headfirst into the sea, the ocean welcomes us in its cool, buoyant arms. The sun shining in our eyes, and the saline waves embracing us; the sand in our hair, and the wind in our face. This is what we live for. This is what makes us cross the forest every single day.

We remain floating over the waves until late afternoon. Then, when the sun threatens to descend into the sea, we make our way out, dress up, and make a mad dash home through the forest.

I don't know if the stories about the bandits were merely stories. That, or perhaps we were too fast for them. Because they never managed to get us. All the stories did was to get us home faster. When I think of it now, it feels like a risk we took back then. But we were young, wild and free. We lived for the thrill.

Coming back to the story, Baa is cooking on the earthen stove—fuelled by logs of wood and coconut waste—when we get back home. We enter through the rear door to make sure she doesn't see us. But the smell of the food tempts and entices us to creep closer.

'How many times have I told you boys to get back home before dark? There are bandits in the forest!' Baa yells at us like a daily ritual.

We tell her we were only playing in the farm. But the sand in our hair gives us away.

'Wait until Bapuji comes home,' she threatens, rubbing her watering, smoke-filled eyes with one hand, and waving a rolling pin at us with the other. 'He will never let you both step out of the house again!'

As I try to reason with Baa, Bhalu picks up two freshly-made chapattis and hides them in his pocket. I reach into the jar of jaggery, grab a fistful, and follow him outdoors.

We sit under the mango trees and devour the chapattis with the jaggery. My brother and I …looking at each other, grinning from ear to ear between our mouths full of food. It is the best feeling in the world, Munnu.

There was something different about the taste of jaggery in those days. It used to be so sweet, malted and flavourful. I don't know what you get these days, but it just isn't the same! If only I could live those days again... that smell of burning wood from Baa's stove. Ah!

Are you paying attention, Munnu? Why do you keep fidgeting with that watch? Sorry? Oh, you are setting it up for your run? What is that beeping sound, Munnu? I won't understand, you say? I must agree. Technology is pretty odd these days. And this old man is getting slow. Yes, I will hurry up. I will not keep you for long, Munnu. But I do want to show you my certificate.

On this particularly beautiful day, Bhalu and I are swimming as usual near the shore. The wind is stronger than usual. It howls in our ears, as if sounding a warning. The waves are much bigger, and we have to leave our clothes further up on the shore, to keep them from getting soaked. Gosh, I remember that day as if it were just yesterday, Munnu!

'Isn't the sea a little unfriendly today?' Bhalu asks me. He is an expert swimmer. He can ride the waves better than a fish. But today, he can't seem to manage his body over the crashing waves. He tries to float, and smack! A giant wave hits him right in the face.

'The sea has never done *that* to me ever before!' he complains, sounding taken aback, and feeling betrayed.

We stay close to the shore, afraid to stray further. But it is no fun staying so close to the beach. So we drop the idea of swimming, and begin to make a giant castle in the sand.

By the time we have to leave, the castle has become such a masterpiece that it hurts to simply abandon it and go home. It is complete with the king's palace, the queen's chamber, the ministers' quarters, the treasury, and the servants' rooms. There is also a garden in front, with a pond in the centre, except that it doesn't have any water because the water we fill in it keeps seeping through the sand. The palace treasury houses a collection of beautiful shells and pebbles, gathered from the beach. And the entire structure is surrounded by a magnificent fortress wall of stones.

All of the fishermen's kids playing in the sand come over to look at our castle. Assuming an air of expertise, and our chests heavy with pride, we give our masterpiece the final touches.

It has taken us five hours to build it. By the end of it, we are exhausted, hungry and severely sunburnt. It is late afternoon, and we ought to get back home, but it is impossible to leave the castle and walk away. Just a few more minutes, we tell each other, and we sit on the soft sand. Bhalu and I hold hands as we admire our castle, imbibing every inch of the beauty of the entrancing structure we built together. Staring at it from different angles. Breathing life into it. Until we get hypnotised and fall in love with it all over again.

The king is delighted with our work, as he walks around in the front garden. The queen is busy in her chamber as the maids help her put on her make-up for the evening banquet. The minister is working in his office, chalking out the war strategy, and the cooks are busy cooking a delicious meal of chapattis and jaggery.

Chapattis and jaggery. Ah. It feels like we are home. There is nothing to worry about now, and we can fall asleep.

The king announces us a reward of ten gold coins from the treasury for constructing such a magnificent castle. We collect our ten shells from the treasury and put five each in our pockets.

It is only now, Munnu, at this ripe old age of ninety, that I realise true happiness lies within the heart. Rewards and accolades are nothing but pebbles on the beach. Are you listening, Munnu? That is such a fascinating piece of wisdom, don't you think? Sometimes I wish I had learnt it sooner.

Back on the beach, we are so exhausted that we fall asleep looking at the wonderful castle against the setting sun. Suddenly, a giant wave leaps up and pounces on us. We jump to our feet. The tide has turned and our clothes are soaked. The castle is wrecked; it lies in ruins before our eyes.

It is a disaster! We are drenched; we will never make it home before Bapuji arrives, and our castle is gone!

Whatever one owns, whatever one builds in life merely turns to sand and dust, Munnu. All that remains is the happiness from the memories one builds in the sands of time.

Bhalu and I are just getting over our loss and are about to start making our way back home when we hear a cry of distress in the distance. Turning around, we see a lady calling out for help, waving her arms, and pointing into the sea. We look closely. A boy our age is struggling against the pull of the tide.

A few fishermen are looking on helplessly. The tide is turning, and there is nothing they can do. If they tried, they would be swept away into the sea, just like the boy.

'Do something, please do something! My boy, my child!' the lady is wailing as the unsympathetic sea pulls him away.

Dazed, I look at Bhalu. 'What do we do?' he asks me, his voice ringing with alarm.

'There is nothing we can do,' I tell him. 'The tide is turning!'

Even a young boy who has grown up by the sea shore will know that when the tide turns, you must stay as far away from the waters as you possibly can. For the turning tide has taken the best of swimmers.

My brother throws me a glance and I know exactly what he is thinking. Now that I am ninety, in retrospect it seems like an impulsive, thoughtless thing to have done. But at that time the blood running through our veins was young and hot, and the brain foolish.

Without losing another second and without batting an eyelid, we run towards the sea like we always do. Only this time, we are doing it for a different reason. The fishermen holler a warning, trying to stop us as the angry sea displays its foamy wrath.

Going against the waves, we try to steer towards the drowning boy. Every few minutes his head emerges from the waters in the distance, only to be pulled under the surface.

Bhalu quickly moves in the lead with swift, efficient strokes. We seem to be doing well until a mammoth wave strikes. It picks up my brother high above the surface of the sea and flings him back with tremendous force. All I see is his head disappearing into the dark waves.

I begin to panic. Is this how it will end? Will I lose my brother, and probably my own life, trying to save someone else's? With all the strength I have, I begin to paddle towards where Bhalu went down. After two gut-wrenching minutes, where life and death keep flashing before my eyes, his head emerges out, gasping for breath. Phew!

We need to get out of here, I think to myself. But somehow, he thinks differently. Now that we are in the sea, the only direction we follow is straight ahead. There is no other way, so we keep swimming.

Moreover, I am in no mood to emerge embarrassed at the beach, with the fishermen dragging us to safety, and us seeming like fools who bit off more than they could chew. Until just a little while ago, we owned the most magnificent castle on the whole wide beach. We couldn't act like losers now.

Saying a silent prayer laced with desperation, the very prayer we say before running through the forest, we begin making our way towards the drowning boy. The waves are strong beyond comparison. Our eyes are blinded with salt water, and our bodies are being flung around by the waves, like a cat playing around with a helpless mouse before pouncing on it. I glance towards the shore. It seems miles away. The fishermen look like tiny dots.

The drowning boy's head starts remaining under the surface for increasingly longer durations of time. Perhaps he is beginning to give up. We paddle more furiously. The rough sea pelts its waves on our faces with all the force it can muster. Salt water fills my mouth and nose, and burns my windpipe.

I look out for the drowning boy's head with every stroke. It bobs up and then goes down again. Instinctively, I start counting in my head. One... Two... Three... Four...

His head remains inside. My heart beats faster. For a moment, I lose my count as a wave throws me up in the air yet again. When I land, I resume counting. He is still inside.

Ten... Eleven... Twelve...

This can't be good. After twenty seconds, his head emerges, almost lifeless.

Sorry? What is it that you say, Munnu? You will have to be a bit louder. You say you don't like the suspense? But that is what happened, Munnu. I remember everything vividly, and I am narrating it to you because I want you to feel what I felt. But you look fretful. Let me cut the story short then. You must really be getting late.

My brother reaches the sinking boy first. He holds his head up, until I manage to reach him. Between the two of us, we keep him afloat. Back at the shore, the fishermen have managed to get a small boat into the water. They begin to steer it towards us. All we need to do is keep our heads, and the boy's, above the water until the boat arrives.

But it is easier said than done. My arms are aching and I feel as if I am paralysed waist down. The boy is showing no signs of life or struggle, and it is one hell of a task to keep him afloat in the stormy sea. I don't know how many times I swallowed mouthfuls of salt water that day, but we manage to hold him until the boat reaches us. The fishermen throw us a rope and we get the boy into the boat.

Once we are on the shore, the fishermen work to remove water from the boy's lungs. After five excruciatingly long minutes, made even longer by the hysterical cries of the mother, he comes back to his senses. His mother breaks down in joy and hugs us both. Bhalu and I are so overwhelmed that we hug each other and begin to cry. It seems funny now, doesn't it, Munnu? But it is this explosive mixture of extreme fright, delight, ecstasy, gratitude and jubilation that brought us young boys to tears. Even though I am ninety now, and have had my share of serious health issues, I must say that day was the closest I have ever been to death, Munnu.

Suddenly we realise we need to get back home. The sun has already set. Bapuji will be reaching home any minute now. Baa is going to be so upset with us today. But the fishermen won't let us go. We are heroes for the day, and we must be taken home like heroes. A special horse cart is called, and with drums beating, we are escorted to the farm. The kind lady even offers us ten rupees as reward for our bravery.

Ten rupees! It was a lot of money back then, Munnu. Enough to buy laddoos that would last a whole damn year!

When we reach the farm, Baa comes out to see what the ruckus is all about. What trouble have the boys gotten themselves into? Then, when she hears what we have been up to, she breaks into a proud smile.

But, Munnu, you know what she tells us once the party of fishermen has departed?

'How many times have I told you boys to get back home before dark? Wait until Bapuji comes home. He will never let you both step out of the house!'

Isn't that such a funny thing, Munnu? When Bhalu was still alive, we would talk about it and crack up every single time!

Alright, Munnu, yes, you can leave now. I won't keep you any longer. You are getting late.

But wait, Munnu, I didn't tell you about this certificate! Later, you say? We should continue the story later? Okay, as you say, Munnu. When will you be back? Munnu?

Munnu?

Oh, you are gone already! I am sorry to have kept you waiting. It was a wonderful story, though, wasn't it? There is still a very interesting part of the story remaining. But you are gone! Never mind. I will wait for you to return to tell you the rest of the story.

***

Dadaji's story keeps playing before my eyes as I begin running towards the sea. It is difficult to believe that the road I am running along on was just a dirt trail in a dense forest when Dadaji was a small boy. It is difficult to believe that Dadaji was ever a small boy!

I make my way over the bridge across the river, and stop for a moment to catch my breath. I lean against the railing and gaze into the grey water as it keeps flowing incessantly. It is amazing to think that this very river flowed when Dadaji was a boy. And this very river must have flowed when *his* Dadaji was a boy. And for generations to come, it will continue flowing just the way it always has. And someday when I am old, I will tell my very own Munnu how I used to go running over this bridge and look into the grey waters below.

I will tell him about how much running meant to me. About how I used to run up the hill to catch the sunrise. About all those evenings I ran by the sea with my eyes on the setting sun. I will tell him about the races I won. About the...

But wait. Munnu says he is in a hurry. He says he needs to go...

Suddenly, an inexplicable sense of emptiness fills me. All that I have lived so far, all the experiences I have been through … they all mean so much to me. All I want to do is share it with someone. Someone young and fresh; someone I love. Like Munnu.

Years will pass, I will grow up, grow old, and then this body will turn to dust. Like Dadaji's castle on the beach. All I can leave behind are the stories I have lived. I remember the words from Dadaji's story. All that will remain is the happiness from the memories you build in the sands of time, he had said.

I look into the grey waters below. My reflection looks funny. The gentle ripples in the water make my face look like it is covered in wrinkles—old and shrivelled, as if I am ninety years old.

I think of the eagerness in Dadaji's eyes and his toothless smile as he told me his story earlier this afternoon. I think of the yellow piece of paper in his hand which had brought back memories that meant the world to him.

I look at my face in the water for the third time. There will come a day when this face will be hidden away behind the old, old lines of wrinkles. When my ears won't hear, my eyes won't see, and my glasses would be somewhere in the bedroom. When my old head would be losing its memory.

There will come a day when I won't be able to lace up and run anymore. A day when the memory that I could once lace up and run will be the only thing that will bring a smile to my toothless face. And then, all I will desire is that my own Munnu draws up a chair and sits next to me. That we sip on mint sherbet in the veranda together. That I show him my certificate. And tell him my story.

I have never cut my run short. But today, I need to. I turn around and run all the way home. As if I am running through a dense forest, one infested by bandits. I am running as if Baa will yell at me if I reached home after sunset. And as if Bapuji will never let me step out of the house again if I got late.

I am running because there are ninety-year-old stories that I need to hear.

***

I reach home, panting hard. Dadaji is sitting in the veranda, smiling dreamily, lost in thoughts. I notice he is still clutching the yellow certificate of bravery in his hand, pressing it close to his chest.

'Oh, you are back, Munnu!' he exclaims, delighted.

'Yes, Dadaji,' I pant, as I bend down to get my breath back.

Dadaji looks at me fondly as I crouch down on all fours. 'Tell me, Munnu, what is that creature that crouches on all fours when young, then on two, and on three when it is old?'

I try to hide a smile as I pretend to think. 'I don't know, Dadaji. What is it?'

'Humans!' Dadaji exclaims triumphantly. 'First we are kids crawling on all fours, then adults on two legs, and then old, like me, hobbling around with a stick!'

'Very clever, Dadaji!' I laugh.

Dadaji laughs back.

'Tell me more about that story, Dadaji,' I point at the piece of paper in his hands.

Dadaji's eyes light up with elation. I have never seen such ecstasy in his eyes before. Or perhaps I have never paid attention to them.

'Draw a chair, Munnu, and sit next to me!' he says, his voice quivering with exhilaration. 'Oh look, I almost forgot, I made mint sherbet for us. I thought you might be thirsty after the run. Come, let us have the sherbet together as I tell you the story!'

I look at Dadaji. For the first time, I notice how charming and charismatic his face looks. And the wrinkles on his face ... It is true, isn't it, that the most enlivening stories of the world are written along the old, old lines of wrinkles.

Maybe that is life's way of passing the stories down generations. Maybe it is life's way of completing a full circle. Or perhaps simply a way to get a man and his grandson to share a drink.

I pick up my glass of mint sherbet, and hand Dadaji his. The twinkle in Dadaji's eyes says it all. The grin on his face looks just as it would have eight long decades ago.

The sherbet tastes heavenly. Dusk surrounds us, and the colours in the sky are spectacular. For a moment, I get lost in its grandeur. Lazy dragonflies buzz around the garden and the gentle breeze sends soft ripples over the water in the lotus pond.

'Draw a chair, Munnu...' Dadaji repeats.

I come back to my senses. I take a seat next to him.

Sipping on the refreshing drink, clutching the old certificate in his hand, a blissful smile resting on his lips, Dadaji shuts his eyes, breathing in the contentment of a lifetime, and takes me back eighty years to when he was a boy.

A boy like Munnu.

***

the bull-tamer

Sometimes in winter, in this little coastal town of Umarsadi, if the night is extremely still and you happen to wake up in the middle of the night and listen intently, perhaps you will hear the gentle roar of the sea in the distance.

When I was a young boy, I used to think it was the sea shivering with cold. When I grew up, they taught me that it was because the air is denser in winters, and hence a better transmitter of sound. But I would like to believe it is both. For you can't simply forget your childhood with all its childish ideas, can you?

And if you are courageous enough to draw out your hand from under the warm blanket and open the bedside window just a little bit, perhaps you will catch the smell of fish on the jet of the freezing night breeze that hits your face. On long horizontal bamboo poles held in place by vertical ones, the fishermen dry their catch by the jagged, rocky beach. It does enough to ward away tourists, and so the town of Umarsadi remains quiet and hidden among the fields lined by several babbling streams that rush to meet the roaring sea.

I still listen to the sea sometimes. Tucked away in my bed on cold, winter nights. Waiting for the alarm clock to go off at five. It is a beautiful sound, isn't it? That timeless rumble. The eternal swish of the waves. Almost an hour seems to pass before the next wave comes along. And sometimes I find myself falling asleep waiting for that next swish to happen.

The sea has kept me company as I run alone. When I am forced to keep away from it because of the hot sun, I run in the shade and the breeze from the sea caresses my face, and I know I am not far from home. It still brings along that stench of dried fish from the shore. It brings the salt to my lips. It seems to merge with the salt from my sweat. And it tells me we are made from the same substance: the sea and I.

Sometimes, when I run along the shore, the floating seagulls flap their wings in alarm as I approach, and then I notice that the dampened sound of my footsteps in the sand matches the flapping of their wings. And I smile to myself. Because it is an incredible feeling to be in perfect sync with the rhythm of the universe.

But every time I hear the sound of the sea, there is one face that comes before my eyes, no matter where I am. Sarfraz.

Because when I was still a small boy playing shells with him, he was the first person who made me hear the sound of the sea merely by cupping a seashell over my ear.

'The entire sea in one tiny shell?' I had asked, my eyes brimming with awe. And Sarfraz had simply smiled and nodded.

The entire village knew Sarfraz as the bull tamer. For me, Sarfraz was the Prince of Persia, my only playmate on the farm, and my best friend in the whole of Umarsadi.

***

'Faster! Faster!' I cry at the top of my voice. The wind is laced with the buoyant smell of warm after-school happiness, and as it rushes through my ears, for those few exhilarating seconds all I can hear is the deafening gush of the breeze riding above my own shrieks.

Sarfraz pushes the cart faster. Carefully, with both hands outstretched to maintain balance, I bring myself to my feet, until I am standing upright, hands in the air, my legs planted firmly on the wooden platform of the zooming cart. And like a master of kinesis, like a hero on a moving train, like the king on a golden chariot, and like a sorcerer on a magic carpet, I stand erect, balancing myself until the cart comes to a slow halt over the bumpy farm trail.

'I am the Prince of Persia!' I exclaim.

'Prinsopersaaa!' Sarfraz repeats, and I have a hearty laugh.

'Say it again?' I ask of him, trying to hold back laughter.

Embarrassed, a visibly red-faced Sarfraz shakes his head sheepishly. He doesn't go to school. How would he know about the Prince of Persia? I explain to the poor lad all I know about Persia—stories from my fantasy, intermittently fortified with tales from the Arabian Nights that Fui, my paternal aunt, reads out to me.

I see his eyes gleam with delight. He especially loves the part where I tell him about the magical flying carpet. Suddenly, he, too, wants to be the Prince of Persia, so he gets on top of our flying carpet and it is my turn to push the cart. He says I have an unfair advantage of the gentle downward slope. I tell him that aided by the slope, I will be able to push the cart faster for him. He seems to consider for a moment, and then finally agrees. Adjusting his skull cap, and clutching the edges of the cart tight, he prepares himself for the ride. I push hard. The gentle downward slope makes it much easier. And the jubilation in his eyes fills me with renewed energy to push harder.

'Baaju! Baaju!'—Move away! Move away!—'Here comes Prinsopersaaa!' Sarfraz yells at the top of his voice, laughing with the wind.

I still remember that clear resounding laughter. The vivid memories of his eyes filled with unadulterated joy. I have never seen such wordless delight play with the wind. So much so that I can't really say what I enjoy more: getting onto the magic carpet and being the Prince of Persia or pushing the cart to make Sarfraz the Prinsopersa. Today, thinking back, I think it was the latter.

The wind puffs up his clothes as his laughter reverberates through the rustling mango trees. I feel the sting of exhaustion from having to push so hard. And for one fleeting moment, it all seems so perfectly congruous, so sublimely tuneful, as if they were all simply meant to coexist—the sound of the wind, that skull-cap wearing lad's resonant laughter, and my heavy panting. As if they were conversing in hushed whispers, speaking of the excited throb of the farm's heartbeat.

I look down and keep pushing harder. The slope carries the cart at breakneck speed, cruising over potholes, flying over rocks, shattering twigs that happen to come in the way. Somewhere far, far away I hear laughter. Sarfraz, I smile to myself. Somewhere far, far away I hear Sarfraz shouting and asking me to stop. Eyes to the ground, I give the cart one last push even as my lungs are about to burst open.

When I look up, the first thing I see is the look of terror on Sarfraz's face. Too late. The cart is rolling at blistering speed towards an open ditch! And holding on desperately to the sides of the cart, poor Sarfraz is screaming at the top of his voice.

'Stop! Stop! Help!' he cries.

I want to do something but my heart is thumping against my ribs so hard that I can barely think.

At the very last second, moments before the cart crashes into the ditch, Sarfraz lets out a horrific cry and jumps off the moving cart, landing face-down on the ground, as the cart disappears into the trench in a cloud of dust.

'Sarfraz!' I yell, my voice shaky.

Nothing. Enveloped by dust, his body lays motionless on the ground barely a foot away from the ditch.

'Sarfraz!' I rush towards him.

Still no movement. Is he dead, I think to myself, covering my mouth in horror. What will I tell his Abba? What will I tell my parents? Tears fill up my eyes. Just as I am about to shake him, Sarfraz jumps to his feet.

'Prinsopersaaa!' he exclaims, and bursts into laughter.

'You... You scared me, Sarfraz!' I laugh; a laughter of relief that turns into a series of unforgiving sobs. I hug him, crying and laughing at the same time, and he hugs me back.

I dust off the dry leaves sticking to his clothes. He has a small wound on his left knee that has begun to bleed. He picks up some dust from the ground and sticks it to the blood. He says dust makes it heal faster. My teacher in school says it is a terrible thing to do, and that he could catch an infection that might warrant amputation of the entire leg. What is amputation, I ask my teacher. Cutting the leg off, my teacher tells me. That seems like an appalling thing to happen, but I don't tell Sarfraz about it, lest I be laughed at. And obviously Sarfraz would know better than the teacher, wouldn't he? Sarfraz seems to be quite well-versed with these things, although I sometimes have a feeling he covers the wound with dust only to hide it from his Abba.

Abba is Sarfraz's father. I, too, call him Abba, because he has the looks of someone who should be called Abba. He owns a chicken shop near the railway station, a few minutes' walk from our farm. While I am away at school, Sarfraz helps his father at the shop. When I return, I see him waiting for me at the gate. I want to throw away my school bag and go play with him. But my mother says I need to change out of my school uniform because I have to wear it again the following day. Every set of uniform must be worn twice before it can be justified for washing. It is the universal law of uniforms.

So I change out of the uniform, have a fresh fruit from the farm—a different one each day that my mother surprises me with—wash it down with a compulsory glass of milk and dash to the gate. I am late, but Sarfraz is still there waiting for me. I heave a sigh of relief. Playtime!

But wait! What is the matter? Just across the road, where we have a cow shed, a small crowd has gathered near the iron gate at its entrance. Curious, we join the group of villagers.

It is Nandi, our bull. Nandi has grown into a full-sized adult now, and off late has been wanting to establish himself as the alpha male. He doesn't let anybody leash him in the shed. Not even Chibu, who has seen him grow up from a small, black-eyed calf that Nandi once was. Nor does he let anybody attach the bullock cart to him. He snorts and kicks up dust, displaying great anger, if anybody tries to get close. He waves his massive horns, threatening to trample anybody who comes his way. Having no work to do but eat all day, he has grown bulky like a wild hippopotamus.

The crowd waits at the gate watching as Chibu tries to lure him with food. But no luck; Nandi shakes his horns angrily if Chibu tries to go closer.

'I will tie him!'

The crowd falls silent as the voice of a child rises over the buzz of excitement from the crowd, and people turn around to see who the voice belongs to. Who is the mouse who thinks he can tame a beast? To my surprise, the owner of that voice is right next to me. I know the voice a little too well. It belongs to Sarfraz.

'I will tie him!' he repeats, even as I tug at his oversized kurta, trying to get him back to his senses.

'He is crazy,' somebody in the crowd mumbles.

'The bull will toss him higher than that tree!' says another.

Somebody laughs.

'We have all tried. Let him try now,' sniggers another farmer.

But Sarfraz is unrelenting. 'I will tie him,' he repeats for the third time.

'I will tie him,' mimics somebody from the crowd in a childish voice that makes the others roar with laughter.

'Sarfraz!' I hiss at him angrily. 'What the hell are you doing?'

Sarfraz pushes me away.

'The bull will kill him!' someone from the crowd shouts.

'The bull will kill you!' I yell back at Sarfraz.

Before I can stop him, Sarfraz is on his way towards Nandi. The crowd parts into two to make way for him. 'Marva de!'—Let him die, someone mutters.

'Sarfraz, are you out of your mind or something?' I shout as loud as I can, hoping Abba will hear me if he happens to be passing by. But neither does Sarfraz turn back nor does Abba emerge from the crowd to save his boy.

'Somebody stop him,' I look around desperately for help.

Nobody stops him. Secretly, they all want to see a small child being tossed into the air by a furious bull. What harm could it do to them? The boy was going to the bull of his own accord, despite everyone's warnings. Serves him right! Besides, they will have a story to pass around in the village.

Nobody bothers to stop Sarfraz, perhaps because he is wearing that skullcap. Because he belongs to a minority community in the village! Oh, those evil hearts!

A confident Sarfraz keeps walking forward. Even Chibu shies away into the shadows. He doesn't want to be blamed for whatever it is that might happen to the boy. In the distance, Nandi shakes his horns as a warning, and the bell on his collar tinkles angrily. A cloud of dust hangs around him, like a looming storm. He snorts loudly, sending ripples of anxious excitement through the crowd. As for me, I am too terrified to see what might happen next.

Sarfraz walks right up to the fuming bull. The crowd holds its breath; I cover my eyes.

And then... nothing. Silence.

No loud snorts. No shrieks. No cries. No kid flying through the air. A murmur begins to gain intensity, and I open my eyes to the most astonishing sight ever. Sarfraz's tiny hand is outstretched. Nandi's beastly head is bowed low. And as he pats the giant bull on his head, Sarfraz smiles the most tranquil smile ever seen on the lips of a warrior.

The crowd gasps with unimaginable surprise, as Sarfraz tugs gently at the bull's collar, and like a perfectly trained pet dog, Nandi follows. The tiny tinkling bell on his collar now emits some sensationally soulful music.

***

'How did you do that?' I ask Sarfraz, still flabbergasted, still wondering if I have woken up from a dream.

We are perched on the tamarind tree overlooking the cowshed. Every few minutes, Sarfraz wedges his foot between two branches, and balancing himself skilfully, reaches out to the tamarind pods hanging all around us. One by one he hands them to me, and turning up the bottom of my T-shirt to form a receptacle, I collect them all. Then we peel open the brown pods, letting the shell fall down from the tree, and begin sucking on the sourness of the tamarind.

But I am hardly interested in devouring the pods. I can't seem to get my eyes off the hero sitting next to me.

'Tell me,' I poke him impatiently in the ribs. 'Tell me, how did you do that?'

'Mmm...hmm...' Sarfraz replies, busy sucking on the tamarind.

'I will push you two extra rounds on the cart if you tell me,' I bribe him.

But somehow, he simply doesn't seem to have an answer. Between two sour bites, he turns to me and smiles. A smile that turns into a wince arising out of the sourness. Then he mumbles something about speaking the bull's language. Something about one universal language of love and harmony. But he can't seem to put it into the right words. It seems from the look on his face that sucking on the tamarind is a lot easier than trying to explain what I am asking him, so I finally give up.

Since that day, Sarfraz came to be known for his amazing bull-taming skills. Every time Nandi misbehaved, Chibu would come looking for Sarfraz. Every time an angry bull stormed the marketplace making people run helter-skelter, they would have one name on their lips: Sarfraz.

My friend seemed to have been born with a special gift. The way snake catchers communicate with snakes in an unknown language that calms the snakes. Perhaps that is the language Sarfraz talks about.

That day, sitting atop the tamarind tree, swaying with the branches in the wind, and listening to the sound of Nandi's bell in the distance, I began to understand that unspoken language that connects everything in the universe to each other. I began to feel it while pushing the cart with Sarfraz on it, while listening to the sound of the sea—a feeling that everything is perfect the way it is. That there is an inexplicable connect amongst all of us. That the rustling of the leaves, the tinkling of Nandi's bell, and the breathing of two young lads sitting on a tree … all resonate with the harmony of the universal frequency.

Of course, back then I was still too young to grasp it all. I could only vaguely feel that emotion. But now that they call me an adult, I am better able to put it into words. Although, in some ironical way, the more I try to express that feeling, the more I feel I am losing grasp of that very special emotion. That maybe I was better off simply feeling it as a child sitting on that branch, sucking on tamarind pods.

The sun looks gigantic from up above. We remain seated in the tree until all the tamarind pods have been consumed, and the only ones that remain are the ones out of our reach. Soon the sea breeze picks up as evening falls over us, and we have to climb down to the safety of a lower, sturdier branch.

At sunset, faraway in the distance, the mullah calls out to the faithful to come and pray. The chants from the nearby mosque fill the silent air. All at once, like a mouse who has just heard a cat's meow, Sarfraz scurries down from the tree with a desperate look of exigency evident on his face. Without a word of farewell or a parting goodbye, he slides down the trunk effortlessly, and races away out of sight.

Abba has taught Sarfraz to pray five times a day. He does that at the mosque each day. Other than that, every time we run to the sea shore to play with shells, we cross the temple on our way. Sarfraz stops for a second, shuts his eyes and slightly bows his head in prayer. Just like any Hindu. As if it were all the same for him. The same God, be it in a mosque or a temple.

From my seat on the branch, as I watch him go, I can't help but notice how much Sarfraz resembles Abba. In his loose, flowing clothes and the skull cap, he looks like a miniature, beardless version of Abba. I watch as his bare feet carry his tiny frame away towards the source of the chants. From top of the tree, his figure looks exceedingly small. I wonder if it was the same figure that had walked up unflinchingly to a beast and patted him on the head.

I shut my eyes for a moment, listening to the muezzin's call. *Allahu Akbar... Allahu Akbar.* The words stretch way beyond my breath can last. The chants flow with the wind. Like the sound of the sea. It all seems so peaceful.

Surely this, too, is a part of that very same universal language, just like the language of the sea, like the tinkling of Nandi's collar bell, like the rustling of the leaves on the tamarind tree, the same language that Sarfraz speaks of…?

It is a beautiful feeling—a feeling that everyone in the world is a friend and a well-wisher. That the whole world is my home. That there are no enemies. That there is nothing to fear.

Oh, how I wish it were true. Because sadly, it isn't. And a few months suddenly change everything.

***

It is another gorgeous spring afternoon at the farm. The trees are laden with mango blossoms and the air is heavy with their fragrance. Butterflies flutter all around the garden, looking for the sweetest smelling flower. The wind feels warm.

I return from school, finish the daily ritual of changing out of my uniform, finish my fruit with a glass of milk, and make my way between the trees and towards the gate in a hurry. But when I get there, there is no sign of Sarfraz.

This is odd, I think to myself. He is never late. What could have happened? Abba might have kept him working for a bit longer, I decide. But thirty minutes later when he still doesn't show up, I start getting agitated. That illiterate fool of a boy! Keeping me waiting! Doesn't even know how to read time!

I decide to go on and play Prince of Persia without him. Serves that fool right! I will tell him how much fun it was, I console myself. I push the cart hard and attempt to swing myself up on top of the moving cart. But however hard I try, it just seems like an impossible acrobatic stunt. Either the cart is too fast, and it drifts away before I can get on top, or it is so slow, it comes to a halt even before I can proclaim myself the Prince of Persia. Frustrated and disappointed, I finally call it quits. I curse Sarfraz for not showing up. Then I decide to climb up the tamarind tree and settle for the brown, pulpy sourness.

But something doesn't feel right. I don't know if it is Sarfraz's absence or that the tamarind pods are simply not juicy enough today. I continue feeling restless. Something has to be wrong, I tell myself. Sarfraz would never miss a single evening.

Across the road, I spot Chibu, and shout out to him. He looks around trying to gauge the source of the sound, then finally sees me perched on the tree.

'Have you seen Sarfraz today?'

Chibu walks closer to the tree, pretending not to have heard me. 'What?' he looks up. Something about his 'what' tells me he doesn't want to answer my question. It sounds vague and uncertain.

'Did you see Sarfraz today?'

'Sarfraz?'

'Yes, Sarfraz.'

He thinks for a moment. And then what he says feels like a dagger pierced right through my chest. For one wild moment, the branch I am sitting on seems to be hacked from underneath me, and I find myself in free fall. 'They left town,' Chibu replies dryly.

***

Abba's shop! I must run to Abba's shop. Quick.

They couldn't have left town. There is some mistake here. How could they have left? Sarfraz was right here with me just yesterday. Surely he would have mentioned it? He loved the farm. He loved playing with me. He would never leave town.

No, Chibu was mistaken. Maybe he didn't hear me right. I am talking about Sarfraz. Sarfraz, the son of... What is his father's real name now? He never told me. Never mind. The son of Abba. Sarfraz, the bull tamer. Who did Chibu think I was talking about?

These thoughts keep spinning in my head as I run towards the railway station. I am out of breath in thirty seconds, but I hurry nevertheless. I must reach Abba's shop. And I must reach there quickly. In five minutes, I am standing before the chicken shop. Or rather, what until yesterday was his shop. For what I see shatters the last bit of hope I was hanging on to. The chickens are gone. The butcher's table lies upturned on the ground. Abba's white plastic chair has its legs snapped apart, as if a storm has passed through the shop. What on earth has happened here?

'Abba?' I shout, trying to keep my voice steady.

No reply. I move a little closer, peering into the open counter window, until the stench of the chickens reaches my nostrils. 'Abba?' Louder this time, my voice quivering.

Still nothing. No sound of movement from inside the little shop. No sign of Abba. No Sarfraz comes running out. Only deadly silence. The stray chicken feathers ruffled slightly by my intrusion. And the old blood stains. As if the entire world had been ruthlessly hacked to death.

The longer I stand there, the deeper the void in my heart becomes. And with every ticking second, the feeling in my gut becomes more and more firm that Chibu was perhaps right, after all. Sarfraz and his family really seem to have left their home.

And the thought fills me with a staggering sense of loss. Of brutal emptiness. As if I was in the middle of a nightmare, and someone had suddenly sucked away everything that I considered happiness in my life, and left me to rot like an empty tamarind pod disposed of from atop the tree. The empty counter of Abba's shop is the last thing I see before tears well up in my eyes and blur my vision.

I begin running back home. I want to get to my mother. The wind feels cold against my cheeks that are streaked with tears. Almost blind from them, and heartbroken from the turn of events, I reach home. Maa holds me close to her and consoles me. Then she tells me what happened.

Somewhere far from our farm, deep in the western part of India, as a train carrying many Hindu pilgrims rumbled through the quiet countryside early one morning, it suddenly caught fire. Many passengers died. Fanatic Hindus began blaming Muslims for the fire. They said Muslims were responsible for torching the train and causing the death of innocent Hindus. That did enough to deepen the already existing rift between Hindus and Muslims; it set off a series of riots between the two religious groups.

I stare back at my mother. I understand nothing. I don't understand what riots mean. It is the first time in my life that I am hearing that word. I couldn't care less about what the Hindus and the Muslims thought. For me, it just meant one thing. And it made me hate the face of religion, or whatever they called it in the world.

Because it cost me my Sarfraz.

***

Time flies. Twenty years pass. I pick up a seashell every now and then and put it to my ear. That perpetual roar of the sea is right there, in a shell. The sound Sarfraz had made me hear. They say a lot changes in twenty years. I don't think I agree. Twenty years … and yet, nothing about the sound of the sea has changed. It is just as soothing as I run towards it today. It seems to call out to me. And the pattering sound of my feet scares away the darkness, as dawn begins to break in the east behind me.

Where did he disappear, I ask the wind that had taken him away. Taken away my playmate. My Prince of Persia. The bull tamer. At least I can be sure that Sarfraz would still be the same person that he was. Something tells me he couldn't have changed. No, not one bit.

I wonder where he would be right now. Will I ever see him again?

My thoughts are broken by the faint clanking of temple bells in the distance. Time for the early morning rituals. Just then, as if perfectly timed by the universe, the mullah's summoning chants rise into the quiet air, in perfect sync with the temple bells. It is a spellbinding rendezvous of sounds. Eloquently stirring music. The temple bells. The mullah's chants. And the roar of the sea. All at once. That one universal language of harmony, I smile to myself. Sarfraz must be close by. Who else could make this happen?

'Sarfraz?' I call out gently to the sea.

And as the winds bring back his reply, the mullah's chants play with an increased intensity in the distance. The temple bells clink louder than ever. A sudden gush of breeze makes the leaves rustle beautifully. Before me, the vast sea roars with the delighted waves.

I come to a halt, breathing in the first rays of the rising sun, with my eyes shut. I place a palm on my chest, feeling the heart thud rapidly against the ribs. It is the same rhythm. The same as the rhythm of the bells. The rhythm of the chants. The rhythm of the wind. The rhythm of the sea.

I smile to myself. 'I am coming, Sarfraz,' I whisper to the wind.

In my palm, I clutch a tiny white seashell just a little bit tighter.

***

the cup of life

He always wanted to meet me. No, not me in particular, but the special man whom his granddaughter chooses. And that happens to be me. And ever since I learnt he is a ninety-five-year-old man who never misses his morning run, I, too, have always wanted to meet Nanaji.

I have spoken to him over the phone numerous times. He has the talent of being able to strike up the most interesting conversation with almost anybody. Consider me, for example. Over six decades between us, and yet when we talk, it feels as if I am talking to a childhood friend. We speak each morning after my run as I walk around barefoot, feeling the cool, dew-covered grass under my feet.

He sits in the balcony overlooking his little garden, reading the newspaper and sipping on chai. 'It isn't just chai,' he tells me. 'It is a cup of life!'

Chai is his all-time favourite drink. I see from where his granddaughter inherits the unyielding fondness for that beverage. I tell him about my run; Nanaji tells me about his. He is an old-timer when it comes to running—doesn't know what distance he runs, has no clue about the pace, doesn't even use a watch. He goes running in his faithful, ten-year-old sneakers under a pair of plain trousers and a cotton shirt. He doesn't know what a ten kilometre race or a half marathon is. He says he has heard of a marathon but doesn't know exactly how long it is. Long story short, one foot before the other is all he understands. He simply runs.

But Nanaji likes listening to how frenzied I am about running. He is someone who seems to understand passion.

He says he is passionate about his work. Unquestionably, he must be. At ninety-five, he still dresses up in the morning, puts on his coat, and goes to court. He doesn't miss a single hearing until lunch. He was a district judge by profession. If you ever speak to him, you would say it couldn't have been any other way. The way he talks, the command in his tone, the modulation in his voice. It is irrefutably a judge's. Even now, looking at his mannerisms, one can almost see the invisible wooden gavel in his hand.

When I tell him how much running means to me, he doesn't laugh like the rest of the world does. He wholeheartedly believes it.

It is a surprise to me, because not many people do. I tell him what kind of a workout I did in the morning. Five times one mile speed intervals at sub 5:20 minutes per mile. He doesn't understand what speed intervals are. I tell him it was gruelling. He tells me I would make the Olympic team if I believe in myself enough. I don't have the heart to tell him I would need to run twice the distance of my longest run at half the pace of my fastest speed intervals, if I am to have a shot at the Olympics.

Over the last eight months and eight hundred phone calls, I have developed a deep affection for Nanaji. And that, too, without having met him yet. 'I can't wait to meet you,' I tell him yet again.

'We will go for a run together,' Nanaji replies. 'But you will have to keep up with the old man!' he chuckles. 'When you are here, I will take you to the court with me and let you sit for a hearing,' he promises. That sounds exciting.

I unlace my shoes and stretch out in the sun. A tiny black beetle climbs over my toes and settles on my foot. Up above, the sky is clean blue. It is a beautiful morning on the farm. I am sure it is even where Nanaji lives. In Raipur. I have never been to that part of India. But now I have a reason to go there: Nanaji.

***

'It is a beautiful morning,' Nanaji's voice comes through. He is back from his run. He says he follows up his run with a cup of chai with some old friends before heading home for another chai. 'Don't tell Nani about the first chai, though!' he makes me promise. 'I am allowed only two cups per day!'

I laugh.

'Oh it's beautiful... It's beautiful...' he exhales slowly. For once, I know it is a consequence of the run. I know it because I feel the same. He groans as he seats himself in his reclining chair and pours himself some tea from the kettle, still holding the receiver to his ear. I can hear the tea trickle out and fill the cup. I wait. I imagine the look of contentment on his face as he inhales deeply and smells the steaming brew. Eyes shut. Just pure pleasure. He sips on the tea with an audible slurp, and exhales a breath of ecstasy. As he sits reclining in his armchair, the scent of the Madhumalti flowers creeping into the balcony from the garden mingles with the aroma from his cup of life. An ancient transistor set on the teapoy next to him reports freshly brewed news. Sunlight streams into the balcony, and Nanaji basks in the warmth of its rays. I visualise an enchanting picture.

No, like I said before, I have never been to Raipur. But I have seen it through Nanaji's eyes. Felt it through his words. The way he describes every little thing around him makes me feel the city throb in my veins. It brings the city right before my eyes. It takes my heart to the city. And brings the city right back to my heart. From what I gather, Raipur seems like a small city, with a charmingly fresh setting.

As fresh as the steaming cup of chai on Nanaji's teapoy.

***

When dealing with Indian Railways, getting a confirmed ticket gives you almost as much happiness as winning a lottery ticket does. After months of waiting, I finally have a train ticket to Raipur. Kavyaa and I will travel together and spend a week with her grandparents. I can't wait to break the news to Nanaji.

'Twenty-four days until we meet!' I exclaim.

He is equally exuberant. 'I will be there at the train station to pick you up.'

'We will go running as soon as I am there!' I remind him.

'Yes, but not before a cup of life!' he smiles.

'Of course!'

I already know what present I am going to take for Nanaji. That afternoon, I open my cupboard and fish out a brown cardboard box tucked away at the back of one of the shelves. I open it carefully, and there they are—gleaming white pieces of crockery covered in bubble-wrap—elegant, graceful. I tear away at the plastic. Exquisite Turkish painting appears on the sides. I had bought the set for myself while browsing through an assortment of articles on display in the Grand Bazaar of Istanbul. But so sophisticated is the design that I just couldn't get myself to use it. I can't think of a better owner for this magnificent piece of work other than Nanaji.

'Twenty-three days to go!' I tell him the following day. 'And I have a surprise for you.'

His excitement, like mine, has only increased.

The days seem to pass by a bit too slowly. As the departure day draws closer, the duration of the phone calls gets longer. 'Just got my Maruti serviced. Now the old man will be at your service,' Nanaji tells me laughingly when we count down to the last five days.

I can't remember the last time I was so excited about a trip. Was it the picnic in school, that first trip without parents? Kavyaa laughs at me because my suitcase is packed five days in advance. 'Calm down, mister. We are simply going to Nanaji's,' she jokes. 'Not to our honeymoon!'

The next day I rush back from my run, and dial Nanaji's number. 'Four days to go... Four days to go!' I am singing aloud even before he answers the call.

The phone keeps ringing, and eventually disconnects.

Where are you, Nanaji! Busy making preparations? I dial the number again. The phone rings for a long time before he finally answers.

'Four days to go, your honour!' I trumpet into the speaker.

'Yes...' That is all he says. The tone leaves me puzzled. His voice sounds muffled and unexpectedly quiet.

'Hello... Nanaji...? Is something wrong, Nanaji?'

'Nah... Nothing... It is just a cold I woke up with. It is going to be fine!'

It is not.

It is four in the morning when my phone rings. It is Kavyaa. Her voice is dreadfully silent. The type of daunting silence that terrorises you. The kind of hush that tells you something is terribly wrong, even before you hear it. Silence, indeed, speaks the loudest.

'Hello? Kavyaa...? Are you there?'

No reply. Just a silent sniff.

'Kavyaa? Is something wrong?' I am losing my patience.

'Nanaji...' One word is all she can utter.

'What about him? What happened?' I ask as my stomach lurches.

Then she finally says it. Her voice is soft. And yet harsh enough to tear into the dead of the peaceful night. And with it, my world falls apart. In a hushed note, muffled with sobs, she whispers in a cracking voice, 'Nanaji is no more...'

***

I gaze out of the closed glass window of the moving train as droplets of rain slide down the surface. Landscape after landscape passes by as the train chugs on endlessly. A moment back I was staring at a range of hills reaching up to the sky in the horizon. Now we are passing through boundless farmlands. Then suddenly there is an unfathomable lake before my eyes. It seems like time has slowed down. Or maybe sped up?

Just like that the scenery passes by in a flash. Just like the time that flies by. Just like that, ninety-five years pass by in a blur. And all that remains are droplets of rain hanging on the glass window. And a suitcase full of gifts on the luggage rack overhead.

The journey feels long. Raipur seems like it is halfway across the globe. And without Nanaji coming to pick me up, it all seems so meaningless. I feel lost. Lost in the ever-changing landscapes. Lost in this endlessly vast world. A world of thoughts, and memories. To think of it, there *are* no memories, for I never got to meet Nanaji. And yet there are so many...

My thoughts are interrupted by the ticket inspector in his black blazer and shining badge. 'Seat number eleven and twelve?'

'Only one passenger, sir,' I reply quietly.

Kavyaa flew to Raipur that very day, four days ago. She didn't think it was a good idea for me to join her. It would be my first time in Raipur with Nani and all the other relatives, and she didn't want me to be a part of the grieving. As much as I wanted to see Nanaji once before they took him away, I reluctantly agreed to stay back and travel by train four days later, as originally planned.

Four days. It seems ironic how a man could pull off ninety-five long years and then simply fall short by four days! Couldn't time just wait for a bit longer? But no, it waits for none. Time is the ultimate, and we are all slaves in the kingdom of time.

Nah... Nothing... It is just a cold I woke up with. It is going to be fine! I keep thinking of the last words Nanaji said to me. Oh, how I wish it really were just a cold. How I wish I could see him at the station like he had promised every day for nineteen days. But no, time did not permit it.

Village after village, city after city, station after station passes by. And all the while I simply stare out of the window, as if in a trance. I think of how much Nanaji wanted to meet me since the time Kavyaa had introduced me to her family. He was anxious at first. Kavyaa told me he hardly slept the first night after she told him about me. Who is he? Is he a nice man? Will he be able to take good care of her? But as time passed and the duration of phone calls got longer, the anxiety slowly turned into eagerness to meet me. Especially because Kavyaa was his only grandchild. Also because Kavyaa didn't have a father. Over the years, Nanaji had been a father and a friend, much more than a grandfather to her. She was the apple of his eyes.

'Take good care of her. She's a piece of my heart!' he would always tell me over the phone whenever we spoke about Kavyaa.

I would like to consider myself as someone who would take good care of that piece of heart. And after all those conversations with him over the phone, hopefully Nanaji felt that way, too. But I can understand how he would have rather met me once and banished his doubts completely. Once. Once before he went away...

Well, I, too, would perhaps want that if I had had a granddaughter, wouldn't I?

I rest my tired head against the cool glass of the window. It is still raining outside. The tiny droplets form right before my eyes and hold on for a while. For a split second, I see the reflection of the landscape outside in every single droplet. The whole world in one drop. And then they slide down the window. I wonder if it is a metaphor for life that I am seeing. A world inside each one of us, until we hold on. But soon it will be time to go. And then we must simply slide away.

My head feels heavy. I realise I have barely slept in the last four days. I can feel my eyelids drooping. I want to shut my eyes. Just for a moment. But I want to stay awake, too. I *need* to stay awake. He is coming to visit me. The suitor. The suitor for my granddaughter.

Are you feeling better, Nanaji, she asks me, running her fingers through my grey whiskers.

Yes, it is just a cold, I reply. I will be fine. But I feel myself sinking.

Nanaji? Wake up, Nanaji! Open your eyes. She starts shaking me vigorously.

I don't understand the panic. It is just a cold. It is going to be fine. I am just tired. But no, I can't fall asleep. He is coming to visit me. I want to meet him. I want to talk to him. I want to see how well he will take care of her. I have things to tell him. I need to tell him she is a piece of my heart. My head is crowding. It feels heavy. My eyelids seem to weigh a ton. It is too much trouble keeping the eyes open. I am just going to shut them for a while. Ah, this feels better. No, wait! I am falling asleep. Can't he come a bit earlier? I want to meet him. But he won't be here until four days. I open my mouth to ask her. Ask her if he can come earlier. But the words fail to emerge. It is all too tiring for this old man.

Are you saying something, Nanaji, she is asking me, her voice muffled with sobs.

No! No! Why is she crying? Don't cry, dear. It will break my heart. It is just a cold. I am only falling asleep. It feels good. But if you cry, I will be shattered. Your tears are like poison to me. Don't cry, dear.

She says something. I can't understand what. Her voice seems far, far away. Wasn't she sitting right next to me? I can't remember. I am too exhausted. Shutting the eyes feels good. I will wait with my eyes shut. Oh, but this heaviness... The darkness is only getting denser. Her voice is going further away. No, don't take her away; she is a piece of my heart.

But something tells me everything will be fine. He is a great guy. I have spoken to him over the phone. Yes, he is a great guy. She is a piece of my heart, but she is also a piece of *his* heart. I can leave her to him. I can sit back and pour myself a cup of life. I can shut my eyes, and fall asleep for a bit.

Her voice is completely inaudible now. The darkness feels complete. I feel complete. The eyes need some rest. I am slipping into deep, deep sleep. And it feels good. Oh, so good. This old man is tired. But content. That man, he is a great guy. Everything will be great. And I can sit back with my cup of life. No! Wait!

All at once, I jerk back into my senses. I am breathing fast. The train is still rumbling through the countryside. The glass window has become warm against my cheek. I straighten myself up. I am still dazed. The dream seemed so real! I can't decide if it was beautifully enthralling or formidably mystifying.

Two hours later, I am still playing the dream over and over in my head as the train pulls into the station, amidst loud clanking of the wheels against the tracks. The words Raipur Junction stand out clearly in bold black against the yellow background of the massive railway signboard.

I am here.

***

The railway station is filled with people. But not the person my heart yearns to see. It makes me feel desperately empty. I just stand there, waiting, hoping against hope that Nanaji will emerge out of the crowd, waving his hands and smiling with glee.

Old man at your service! Maruti is waiting! he would say.

No. It doesn't happen. I drag the luggage outside, navigating through the crowd of happy people. I seem to be the only one walking with slow steps and shuffling feet. With a little help from a stranger, and a lot of help from a rickshaw puller, I finally make it to Choubey Colony. With little pain, I locate the house. And with a lot of pain I stand before it.

It is just how I had imagined it to be. Except that everything is dreadfully silent. Two cars are parked outside the gate and two inside the driveway. There are still visitors at home, it seems. Nanaji's old Maruti sits in the open garage. Serviced. Washed. But pitifully lonely.

I stand outside the gate for a long time, staring at the nameplate and the letterbox, mustering the strength to lift up the latch and swing the gate open. I can't. I am out of words. Out of expressions. And brimming with inordinate emotions.

There is a concrete seating around a giant Peepal tree outside the gate. I sit down next to my luggage. I call Kavyaa outside. I am not ready to meet everyone yet, I tell her over the phone. I hear the front door click open gently. Kavyaa emerges, walks through the driveway, and out of the gate where I am seated. She is dressed in a plain white kurta. Her long hair is tied in a bun. Her face looks pale and colourless. I envelope her in my arms. She breaks down, leaning against my chest. I can't utter a word. I am clenching my jaws together in an intense effort to fight back tears. I know I need to be strong. I hold her tight. She holds on to me, as if I am all she has. We sit there for a while in silence, neither of us finding the courage to talk. Then, gathering my luggage and her composure, Kavyaa takes me in through the back door and straight to her room. On the way, I spot Nanaji's balcony. The Madhumalti flowers creep inside from the rooftop, just as he had described, but the empty armchair bears a forlorn look. The ancient transistor set is appallingly quiet. There is no steaming kettle, and the cup of life is empty.

It is a terrible sight. The air around me feels agonisingly heavy. The silence is ghastly. I want to see Nanaji. I want to talk to him. But I can't. All I can see is a silent photo frame with his portrait, adorned with a brown garland of dried flowers. And an oil lamp burning before it. I want to cry. And yet I need to hold myself together before Nanaji's piece of heart. I need to be alone for a while to digest it all. I need to find my equilibrium. I need a vent. However loathsome it may sound, somehow it seems the only sensible thing to do is to go running. Over miles that I have run all these years, I have come to realise that I don't just run to keep fit. Or because it feels good. Running is where I find myself. It may sound bizarre, but to me, there is no better time to discover yourself than when you are down to your worst. Beaten down. Panting. Sweaty. Exhausted. Vulnerable. Running is my meditation. My freedom. And that is exactly what I need right now.

I ask Kavyaa to check if it is safe to head out. I don't want to be seen going out for a run. It might be considered offensive or disrespectful, even atrocious, given the circumstances. But at that moment, to me, there is nothing more sacred than lacing up and sweating it out.

We will go running together. Nanaji's promise echoes with my hollow footsteps, as I lift up the latch and walk out of the white gate.

***

I know nothing about Raipur. I don't know a single street here. I don't know where I am going. I keep running along a broad road that passes by a couple of colleges. The good part is everyone seems to know Choubey Colony, and so the chances of getting lost look slim. My mind continues to wander. From the phone calls months ago, to *the* phone call four days ago. From the strange dream on the train, to Nanaji's empty teapoy in the balcony. I feel the sting of tears in my eyes. But I hold myself back.

I pass by rows of government buildings. Some shabby and grey, others proud and white. Then I pass by an impressive-looking building surrounded by tall walls. Could it be a court, I ask myself. *I will take you to the court with me, and let you sit for a hearing,* Nanaji had said. Would this have been that court?

Without a warning, emotions swell up inside me. There is no reason to hold back, I realise. No need to put up a strong face. The sentiments suddenly reach a threshold, and I collapse. And just then the rain comes down. As if it had been waiting, too. It starts with a few drops, then a drizzle, and soon makes the people on the streets scurry for shelter. Only I keep running; running like a madman, tears pouring down like a waterfall. The mirth of the rain mingles with the gloom of the tears. The drops hang on for a while and then slide down my cheeks. A whole world in every drop. A world full of mirth. And a world full of gloom.

I run hard, pant harder, sob even harder. Until the tears completely blind my vision. And then I stop. I am still outside the tall walls of the court compound. Nanaji would have been here. As much as I wanted to go running with him, he wanted to take me to court. As much as I wanted him to experience my passion, he wanted me to experience his.

I run along the compound wall. It seems never-ending. It seems hard to believe that I will never come here with Nanaji. It seems hard to believe that Nanaji isn't here, behind these great walls today. He must be, I decide. For death can't keep you from following your passion, can it?

Twelve kilometres go by. The harder I run, the better it feels. The mind is calming down. Thoughts become scarce. There is not much I am able to think. Concepts in the head have become fewer in number and lesser in intensity. Emotions are a lot milder. As if I happened to pop some soothing pill. But that eternal feeling of heaviness is still paramount and omnipresent. It is dragging me back. Painfully. Squeezing tears out of my heart. Nobody will understand the bond we shared in this short while; nobody but two people. And now, one of them was no more; and the other one is running through the streets of Raipur all alone.

I pass an old man walking with a young lad. They are laughing and talking. And laughing again. That could have been us, I tell Nanaji bitterly.

That *is* still us, Nanaji replies. I am in your heart, like you are in mine. You know what the worst thing is, though, Nanaji asks.

What?

That you are feeling miserable. You are broken. Do you think I would ever like to be the reason for such misery? Nanaji falls silent.

No! Of course not!

Don't cry, dear! I will be shattered. Your tears are like poison to me! Hadn't he said that sometime? I try to recollect. When was it? Yes! In the dream, on the train ride to Raipur.

It suddenly makes sense. When throughout your life, all you have wished for is to see your loved ones happy, how dreadfully harrowing would it be to see them weep as you die! In the kingdom of time, no wishes are granted. Else

Nanaji would have only wished to live on. Even if it was just for four more days.

I try to raise my spirits for the sake of Nanaji. I don't want him to blame himself for the air of melancholy in the empty balcony. That is the least I can do for him. The Turkish earthenware, the lofty plans, the runs, the court hearings ... they will all remain a hollow fantasy, an unfulfilled dream. But seeing Nanaji smile? I could make that happen!

Mile after mile, stride for stride, for one hour we run together through the city: Nanaji and I ... through bazaars, over bridges, through parks and along court compound walls. We trot along together. In perfect sync. In perfect silence. Only when I enter Choubey Colony do I realise that among the hundreds of phone calls and hours of talking, this was the most special conversation I had had with Nanaji.

***

A light drizzle is bathing Choubey Colony in tender morning freshness. The smell of the wet soil fills the garden with a faint, childlike smile.

We sit in Nanaji's balcony, as the Madhumalti flowers blossom above us. The old transistor is reporting news with undiminished enthusiasm, but at a much softer volume to keep the tender patter of the raindrops intact. Nani is sitting in the reclining chair, dreamily looking at the gentle blanket of rain washing over her rose plants. Kavyaa and I sit on either side of Nani, with warm cups enveloped in our palms. Opulent Turkish painting strokes show on the sides of the cups. A steaming kettle sits gracefully on the teapoy.

Don't tell Nani about the first chai! Nanaji whispers to me. *I am only allowed two cups per day!*

Yes, your honour, that is our secret! I wink back.

I look at Nani. A soft smile is apparent in her eyes. She knows about the extra cup already, it seems.

There, sitting in the balcony, looking at the rain, I feel complete. I have pieces of heart to take care of, Olympic teams to make, and secrets to keep from Nani. But right now, I am content.

It will all be great, just pour yourself a cup of life, Nanaji breathes in my ear, and disappears into thin air.

I smile. I know it will all be great. I realise when I am ninety-five, this is exactly how I would want it to be. When it is time for me to bid goodbye, this is exactly how I would want the picture to look like. When the time comes for me to slip down the glass window like a raindrop, when my head feels heavy and I can't keep my eyelids open, it would suffice to know this much. That somewhere in the world, there exists someone just as young, all alone on a train, looking outside to see the whole world in a drop of rain. Someone with that same eagerness in his eyes to meet me. Someone with Turkish crockery carefully gift-wrapped in his suitcase. Someone who can keep the balcony brimming with the aroma of Madhumalti flowers and boiling tea leaves. Someone who can hold my piece of heart close to his own, until the time comes for *him* to slide down the glass window and into an eternal sleep. And then I can sit back and pour myself a cup of life.

The maid loads the suitcases in the trunk of the old Maruti. A young couple and an old Nani take the passenger seats as Nanaji gets behind the wheel. He looks into the rear view mirror, straightens his coat and smiles back at us. He can tell from the aroma. The cup of life is filled up to the brim.

***

the best
life ever

Embedded deep within the folds of the dark brown, rocky mountain ranges of the Spiti Valley, like a startling splash of lush green, a small grain of a village called Rumste sits sleepily in the freezing shade of the monumental Himalayas under the crystal clear skies.

It is 4 degrees Celsius at 7.30 in the morning, and I can only see one peak towering over me, beckoning me to conquer it. You can't get there running, they had told me the previous evening. You can never challenge the might of a mountain.

Oh, I loved it when they said that! I love it when they say you can't do something because it is impossible! It makes me want to prove them wrong. Don't we all want to do that—do the impossible; chase things that the world says are beyond our reach. That is what the human ego is all about.

My host looked at me with panic-stricken eyes. Almost as if I had sinned with those words; as if I had insulted the God of the mountains, and he simply couldn't stand it. 'Ambition is one thing, sir,' he told me, fighting hard to keep his voice from displaying that slight hint of anger. 'And over-confidence is another. And sometimes we don't realise when we cross that fine line.' He had left it at that, hoping that better sense would prevail upon me.

But it hadn't. There was nothing to contemplate; I am a marathoner, after all, I had thought to myself. I am used to being on my feet for long hours, pushing my limits. I will run to the top of the mountain. It shouldn't be a problem. And so, early in the morning, I set out.

The air feels dry and cold. So much so that it stings the inside of my nose when I breathe. I follow the trail with my eyes. It disappears halfway into the barrenness of the mountains. It is probably the fresh air that pumps me up. Or maybe the unfathomable beauty of my surroundings, aided by my greed to get an even better view from the top. But secretly, it is the urge to pitch my sinews against the might of the mountain that gets me here: to prove that I am stronger than the mountain.

A sinister smile dances on my lips as I take the first step—bold and impudent, almost intruding. The cold breeze hits me head-on, but I push against it. It is a mere gust of wind, but it plays its games alright. My ears go numb. A stinging kind of numb. As if an invisible hand is pinching them hard. I clench my fists and keep running.

My eyes begin to water. I blink away the tears. It takes only a couple of minutes and a few hundred metres for me to begin doubting my own capabilities that I had been so sure of just a few breaths ago. But I am in denial. The ego, they say, is mightier than the mightiest mountain.

And before I know it, my heart rate is soaring. My mouth begins to salivate. I suck in lungs-full of air. A deep breath: the best solution to any problem. But no, not here. Not at 13,000 feet above sea level. Ground rules don't work here and breathing in doesn't help. Because it feels I am only breathing in fire.

One kilometre into the run, I stop and bend over, panting furiously, eyes snapping shut. I am confused, surprised, rather shocked. I run seven days a week, triple-digit miles a month. I don't double over panting in the first kilometre. I had known running would be difficult here, but just one kilometre? It is an embarrassment to my legs.

But the fire in the lungs is savage and viciously unforgiving. I turn around to look. The tent where I spent the night, the stream that babbled all night are both gone. The bonfire pit is gone, too. How could one kilometre change so much around me? I am surrounded by mountains—enormous and haughty—looking down sarcastically at their prey. Laughing. Laughing at the feeble, panting creature with famished lungs. It is like running through a nightmare. I panic for a moment. What will I do if I don't find help? The isolation fills me with apprehension.

But the longer I pause, the colder I get. The icy needles of the Himalayan winds are piercing through my bones. I can't run, but run I must. If nothing else, simply to keep warm. And I am not ready to submit. No, not yet. I start off again, slower this time.

The might of the mountains is overwhelming. I look up at the peak. It seems far, far away. Worse still, it seems to be moving away as I run towards it. Was this some callous conspiracy? A cruel joke?

I slow down further to a walk. If I can't run, I will walk. When I can't walk, I will crawl. But give up I won't. I will do whatever it takes to scale that peak.

My mouth begins to feel strange. I taste bile. And lots of saliva. As if I am about to vomit. As I jog slowly, I try to banish the taste. I spit. To my disgust, the wind slamming into my face brings my spit back to me. It lands on my chest.

'Whenever you want to spit at the world,' my mother always quotes a Gujarati saying, 'swallow up your anger. And if you must spit, first spit at your own self a hundred times over.'

Now the mountains are teaching me the same lesson, destroying my ego bit by bit, making me spit at my own self.

I keep walking, suddenly feeling like a speck before the majestic mountains. My intent, my goals, and my purpose in life, all seem so minuscule today. My dreams and aspirations that I so proudly parade are suddenly so diminutive. The feathers that I don on my marathoner cap for the world to see, seem like worthless blades of grass. I don't know for how long, but consumed by thoughts, I keep walking.

I begin to lose track of time. It could have been an hour since I started. Two, perhaps. The body is giving in. My legs ache. My head feels heavy. For the last time I look up at the peak. It still seems just as far away. As if I hadn't moved an inch. As if all this while, as I waged a bloody battle against the mountain, it just slept there peacefully. Like the war hadn't even started on the other side. I suddenly feel inconsequential. And I am shattered.

I sit down on a rock and shut my eyes. My head is spinning. I am breathing hard. I am unable to think. The lack of oxygen finally seems to have hit me. The back of my head feels like it will blow up. The roots of my fingernails seem to have turned blue. Or is it simply my imagination? My eyes refuse to open. No amount of air that I suck in seems to help with the breathlessness. As if I am merely breathing in vacuum.

Am I dying?

I am too drained to answer that; too exhausted to even panic. I just want to be left there lying on the rock, eyes shut, gasping for life.

And all the while, the mountains stand unmoved. I am overcome by a strong sense of intimidation. Here I am, dying before them, and they simply observe? If I die here, will these prodigious mountains bother? Will the world care? Let alone the Himalayas, will even a grain of sand move to cover my body? Will the clouds cry even one drop of rain over me?

My ego collapses. Once and for all. In those blurry moments, I am reminded of my host. His faint, unclear face appears against my shut eyelids. He was right. There is ambition. And then there is the ego. And all this while I had been trying to wreak havoc in the land of ego. What I didn't know was that it was also the land of self-sabotage.

I don't remember how long I lay there: Walking over the fence between my imagination and reality, drifting in and out of sleepy illusions, until the incessant beeps from the stopwatch bring me back to my senses.

I don't know if it is a result of my thoughts or of the rest I got, but I feel different. I open my eyes. I realise I am crouching before the massive mountains, bowing down before them. Because they finally brought me down and made me surrender. The words my host had spoken come to me like a sudden realisation. 'You don't ever conquer a mountain, sir,' he had said. 'You are merely permitted to stand on it!' For the first time, I understand what he meant. And I am suddenly grateful I have the permission to cower like a mouse before the majestic mountains.

I am lost. Slowly I rise to my feet. Head bowed low, I glance ahead along the trail. I don't want to look at the peak. I can't. I don't deserve to. But I believe I can run the next few steps. And that would be a good enough reason to rise.

Belief, they say, is empowering. And faith moves mountains. I can't speak for the mountains anymore, but it does move me. It moves me enough to get me to my feet. One thing is clear. To run here, I couldn't compete against the mountains. I had to be on the same team. I had to be the speck, the dot, the molecule that I was. I had to be myself. One step after the other, I start running. One foot before the other. In the middle of nowhere. Towards nowhere. Feeling vulnerable as ever. And yet, strong enough for the next step.

I smack the stopwatch shut. No longer is this a race. I don't need the kilometre splits or the average pace. The mountains couldn't care less about my cadence or my heart rate. This is purely about the joy of running. It reminds me of the days when I used to run as a child through the farmlands. Sometimes in slippers, at times barefoot. Chasing goats sometimes, and sometimes simply for the joy of being alive, for the joy of running. And so, I keep running along the giant mountain ranges.

The two other farm kids have stopped under the chikoo tree. I run to get the sweetest chikoos before they are taken. The sun is setting. The sky is orange. And the golden-brown chikoos are deliciously juicy.

I don't know how far I have run now. It could have been a few minutes. Maybe a few miles. The cold, rocky desert is never-ending. I don't want to turn back. Just a few more metres. Just until the next bend in the road. Just to see what it looks like there. Just for the pleasure of it. I don't want to stop. I can't stop. I am panting furiously. And yet floating effortlessly. Like I am gliding through a dream. Putting in the effort, but not feeling the pain. Running through a tantalizing brew of lava-hot ice. Running through a misty haze of thoughts. Through a beautiful trance.

I am tired. My eyes are zoning out. I am staring into the distance at nothing in particular. The trail seems to be all uphill. But then, if I imagine it to be otherwise, it instantly goes all downhill. This is good. It is all in the head.

I hear somebody call my name. I stop and look around.

Nobody. Only the persistent stillness. And the sound of the wind.

I cup my hands. 'Who is it?' I call out.

Nothing. Silence.

Only the mind playing its games. I keep running, waiting for someone to call me again. But it doesn't happen.

Pockets filled with ripe chikoos, I run back home, as the crimson rays of the dying sun light up the garden pond. I can smell coconut oil in the air. Maa is frying puris. I take a seat on the kitchen platform, cross-legged, waiting for the first lot to emerge from the hot, bubbling oil.

I hear some sound again. This time it doesn't stop. As I run around the next bend in the trail, I see a group of Buddhist monks clad in maroon and orange, sitting around a makeshift stone stupa, chanting.

Om-MaNi-Padme-Hum

The chants are melodious. They sync with the rhythm of my footsteps as I run by. The tune keeps ringing in my head, long after it becomes inaudible to the ears. It seems to match my breath. Until my breathing becomes one with the chants. With my steps. With the beat of my heart.

In. In. Out. Out.

Left. Right. Left. Right.

Om. MaNi. Padme. Hum.

It resonates with the rhythm of the universe: one beat, one rhythm, one life, one soul, one entity. And it is all inside me. It is a powerful feeling. I am the mountains. And the mountains are me. I try to channelise my thoughts. I realise I have none. The harder I try, the harder it gets. The void in my head only gets deeper.

The song that mom sings in the kitchen as she fries puris is so soothing. The smell of the puris is so enticing. I wish this would go on forever. The song. The frying.

Om. MaNi. Padme. Hum.

Om. MaNi. Padme. Hum.

The chanting strangely seems like Maa's voice. The melody is etched in my memory. I wonder if she would remember that song. I wonder if I would ever hear it again. I wonder if puris would taste the same ever again.

The eyes well up. I break down. Memories from the past don't make me cry. But today is different. The sky is blue. Like it used to be at the chikoo farm. I miss Maa's song. I miss the puris. The emotions are just overwhelming. I can't help but get nostalgic.

The sobs are choking me. The crying makes it difficult to breathe. The tears filling up my eyes are blinding me. I stop running. Leaning on a rock, I try to stabilise myself. As I turn around to look beyond the edge, a gasp escapes my mouth. The view is breathtaking.

The black rocks jutting out of the white snowy blanket far away in the horizon look like blots of ink on a plain white parchment. I wonder what stories they are trying to pen down before me. Life is all about ink, isn't it? Years from now, I will be dressed in wrinkles, walking into the sunset with trembling feet; my heart will be smeared with blots of ink from the stories I tried to live. And the little stories that defined my life will flash before my eyes one final time. Because it is the stories we live for, and it is the stories we shall die with. And one day, my body will turn into mere words, and the bones will become letters. And the stories I lived—those immortal ink blots—will live way past the sunset, and into a fresh new sunrise. What, then, will my ink say?

My heart begins to race. I can see those stories in ink right there, written over the white sheet of snow.

I can feel the blue skies from the countryside with my eyes shut.

I can feel the sweet juice from a ripe chikoo trickle down my elbow.

I can smell the puris.

I can hear Maa sing. It is the sweetest song ever.

Like a bolt from the blue, it dawns on me. It is not the mountain we conquer, but ourselves!

In one single moment, in the space of one breath, in one blink of an eyelid it strikes me like a spark of divine enlightenment. They coalesce into one realisation. That this moment—this life—that I am fortunate enough to live is beyond a shadow of doubt... the best life ever!

Far ahead, towering high in the sky, the mountains, with all their majestic benevolence seem to be smiling down over me. And call it a play of illusion or an enchanting consequence of living the best life ever, but as I shut my eyes, savouring the sensational moment, for a split second I believe I see the celestial peak bow its proud head gracefully before me.

***

Praise for the Book

'...an authentic, raw and honest story collection from a runner, about what really matters in life...'

- HENRIK WESTERLIN, International Trail runner, Member of Danish National Team

'The descriptions are so magical and mesmerizing; they'll transport you to another world...'

- PRABHA YADAV, MD, Yog Power

'So enchanting... the book will make you smile and cry at the same time!'

- DR. ARTI DASTIDAR, Laparoscopic Surgeon, Mental health & wellbeing counsellor

'The Murakami of India... with writing so fresh, so intense, so profound...'

- JAGJIT SINGH ARORA, Director, VMware

'Through quaint coastal towns and over high mountain ranges; through coconut groves and straight into the heart. This was the best life ever!'

- NAVEEN MV, Group MD, First Agro Japan

About The Author

Shroff holds a bachelor's degree in Engineering from the University of Mumbai. After passing college with a distinction, he gave up a prospective career in the corporate world, and made a life changing decision to move back to a simple, minimalistic farm life, follow his passions—running and writing, and focus on what he calls—the finer things in life.

Shroff spent most of his formative years on his parents' farm in the countryside, running around the never-ending fields "chasing goats and feasting on fresh farm-fruits". This greatly influences his style of writing, which often drifts from the narrow bougainvillea-flanked trails, and over beautifully nostalgic reminiscences. Shroff blogs as The 5 AM Guy and his stories have also appeared at an international level, featuring in inspirational magazines.

Website: www.The5amGuy.com

Facebook: facebook.com/The5amGuy

Twitter: @shroff_aditya

Instagram: @The5amGuy

Write to Aditya at: shroff@the5amguy.com